ADVANCE PRAISE FOR *FROM CHAOS TO CALM*

"In *From Chaos to Calm*, Tamara Kiekhaefer distills decades of clinical experience into a powerful six-step strategy designed to conquer anxiety. This workbook goes beyond theory, offering practical techniques and exercises that readers can implement immediately. Tamara's compassionate and clear guidance makes this an indispensable tool for anyone looking to manage anxiety and regain control of their life."

—Lisa Marranzino, LPC

"Ms. Kiekhaefer's book, *From Chaos to Calm*, is an exceptional read. It synthesizes anxiety from development to life restrictions to treatment, giving the reader powerful tools to use today. She provides clear and concise examples and proven techniques to reduce anxiety for a healthier life.

This gem wastes no time. Strap yourself in and feel better for the long term."

—Laura A. Schroder, LPC

FROM CHAOS TO CALM

A SIX-STEP STRATEGY TO BREAK THROUGH ANXIETY

TAMARA KIEKHAEFER

LCSW

POST HILL PRESS

A POST HILL PRESS BOOK
ISBN: 979-8-88845-944-7
ISBN (eBook): 979-8-88845-945-4

From Chaos to Calm:
A Six-Step Strategy to Break Through Anxiety
© 2025 by Tamara Kiekhaefer, LCSW
All Rights Reserved

Cover design by Cody Corcoran
Editing by Bonnie Hearn Hill
Workbook inserts by Desiree Grimaldi

Post Hill Press
New York • Nashville
posthillpress.com

Published in the United States of America
1 2 3 4 5 6 7 8 9 10

To my husband, my rock and constant source of love and support. Your unwavering belief in me has given me the strength to chase my dreams and create this book.

To my kids, my greatest inspiration. You remind me daily of the beauty and possibilities in the world. Your love fuels my passion to help others find their own peace and happiness.

To my family, who have always been my foundation. Your encouragement and understanding have been my guiding light.

This book is for all of you, with all my love and gratitude.

—Tami

If you are experiencing significant distress, anxiety, or other mental health challenges, please seek support from a licensed mental health professional. In an emergency, contact a healthcare provider or crisis hotline immediately.

The author or publisher are not liable for any consequences arising from the use or misuse of the information provided.

CONTENTS

TAME ANXIETY, UNLEASH YOUR POWER

MY HEART WAS RACING, and I could barely breathe. I was shaky, and my thoughts were bombarding my head. *What if…But then what…I might never…He might always…* blah-blah-blah.

I looked at the clock in my tiny, blistering hot apartment and it said it was 2:42 a.m. The sun wouldn't even be peeking out for four more hours. *I don't think I can take this stress*, I thought. So, I gathered my shoes, a hoodie, my purse, and my keys. I couldn't sit still; I had to go…somewhere. There I was in Palm Desert, CA, barely knowing anyone, hardly knowing the town at all. I'd been there for six months, having moved with the love of my life at twenty-one years old, thinking I was ready for that type of thing. Six months later, it ended, and I was filled with anxiety and heartache.

I jumped in my '66 Mustang and started driving around. No one was on the roads, and every song reminded me how sad I was. I turned on a Spanish music station, because at least I couldn't understand the words. I wondered how other people were able to find and keep love. My heart wouldn't stop pounding, and I couldn't catch my breath. God, I felt like I might die.

Driving without direction, I came up to a Walmart, the only place open twenty-four hours a day. *Ah—I'll go shopping.* But at twenty-one, I was flat broke and couldn't afford anything. *Who cares? I'll just browse around and try to distract my brain.* That's what you do when you're desperate.

Wondering if I'd truly gone mad, I found myself in the shoe department at three a.m. lacing up tennis shoes. You read that correctly. Good God, what a hot mess I was. But when you are in the middle of a panic attack, everyone is a hot mess. At the time, I had no idea what was happening. I was just doing anything to keep my head together.

Fast forward thirty years later, twenty-two of which I'd spent as a psychotherapist working with people with anxiety, depression, relationships, grief, trauma, and domestic violence. I'm writing this book because, not only do I have a ton of personal experience dealing with anxiety, but I want to continue to help people learn the simple, immediate steps to manage their own anxiety.

Once I realized that it doesn't really matter what situation I'm in (because anything can trigger panic and make it hard to think clearly), I understood the importance of taking control of my symptoms. It all comes down to finding ways to manage and alleviate those symptoms. Whether it's a big or small issue, the key comes down this:

- Regaining composure
- Reducing the impact of the symptoms
- Restoring a sense of control

By learning how to navigate and address these symptoms, I help people empower themselves to face any challenge with greater ease, resilience, and clarity of mind.

You may still be asking though, "Why are we dragging the anxiety beast out of its slumber? Isn't it easier to just avoid it?" At this moment, you may be all snuggled up in your bed, ready to fall fast asleep, looking for some type of validating, self-help, pick-you-up, chill out reading. But here you are, reading this. Good for you, I say! If we don't talk about all the emotions and parts of anxiety, they won't go away, I promise you that. Anxiety does not fix itself. It festers and grows and hides in corners until bam, it smacks you in the face. Because if we don't talk about it, it will continue to control you, wreaking havoc in every crevice of your life. Because that's what anxiety does.

SCRATCHING THE SURFACE

Let's dive into the world of anxiety—the ups, the downs, the ways it can fuel us, and the moments it can feel overwhelming. Together, we'll shine a light on this topic and explore every aspect of it. By openly discussing and dissecting anxiety, we can gain a deeper understanding and find strategies to overcome its challenges. Don't worry, though—amidst the complexities, there is always hope. Through knowledge, support, and empowerment, we'll navigate the journey toward learning to take control of our anxiety and reclaim a sense of peace and fulfillment. So, let's gather around the table and unravel the mysteries of anxiety, discovering the power within ourselves to create a brighter, more resilient future.

Now is the time to act. Now is the time to learn how to get the upper hand and squeeze the power and control out of the aspects of anxiety that don't serve you.

With deep compassion and a burning desire to make a difference, I have poured my heart and soul into this book. It is my heartfelt mission to shed light on the intricacies of anxiety, unveiling its origins, unraveling its complexities, and exploring the profound impact it has on our lives. I want to reach out to as many people as I can, offering a guiding hand to those who have been trapped in the clutches of anxiety for far too long.

Through these pages, I aim to provide you with a clear understanding of anxiety—what it truly is, where it stems from, and why it manifests in our lives. But it doesn't stop there. My ultimate goal is to empower you with a strategy that is *clinically proven* to help you take control of your anxiety, to break free from its grip, and to reclaim a life of freedom, joy, and fulfillment.

In my first book, *Preparing for the Jungle: Avoiding Snakes and Pitfalls on the Path to Healthy Love*, I briefly touched on how anxiety can be a learned behavior based on the theory of attachment. I talked about how unhealthy communication and conflict resolution can contribute to low self-worth and how anxiety is a product of such experiences. While that book primarily focuses on empowering you to achieve success in romance, it also weaves in strategies for overcoming anxiety throughout its pages.

After that book was published, I realized that the topic of anxiety deserved its own bound dedication. Why? Because no one should have to face the overwhelming weight of anxiety alone. Together, we can embark on a transformative journey, equipping you with the knowledge and skills needed to navigate the challenges, manage the symptoms, and ultimately find solace in the face of anxiety.

I know firsthand the struggles and limitations that anxiety can impose on our lives, but I have also experienced the power of healing, resilience, and personal growth. It is my sincerest hope that by sharing my insights, experiences, and research, I can provide you with a roadmap toward a brighter, more vibrant future—one where anxiety no longer dictates your every move.

I hope that you find value in each page. I hope you take the time to be completely honest with yourself as you use the questions and self-reflection to learn about who you are. I also hope that you implement each action step into your daily life. Please don't let this book become a dust collector on your shelf. Use it as a reference guide. Anxiety comes in all shapes and sizes. It shifts as we get older. I hope that you choose to not let fear dictate your ability to be happy and find internal peace. My greatest wish for you is to have a few—okay, a ton of—aha moments. If you find as much value as I think you are going to, I only ask that you to commit to spreading the word, share my book, and share what you learn.

So, let's embark on this journey together. Let's break down the barriers, dispel the myths, and cultivate a sense of hope and empowerment. I am here to guide you every step of the way, offering support, understanding, and a genuine commitment to your well-being.

Together, we can rewrite the narrative of anxiety, forging a path toward a life defined by strength, resilience, and the unwavering belief that you have the power to overcome and thrive.

HOW TO USE THIS BOOK

The book is designed with purposeful sections that require your time and attention. Each section is meant to resonate and be absorbed, so take your time and do the work. Allow the information to become ingrained as you form new habits. Implement what you are learning every day and document your thoughts and reactions through this process. Remember, you are shifting old patterns and habits and replacing them with techniques that work.

It's important to note that this book complements but does not replace individual therapy. If you find yourself emotionally or mentally challenged and struggling, please consider seeking professional help. With opportunity ahead, prepare yourself to dive in, grab your favorite journal and pen, and get determined for growth. I wish you strength, light, and love on your journey. I am here with you.

Tame your anxiety, unleash your power!

CHAPTER ONE

DECODING ANXIETY - EXPLORING THE ROOTS

WE'VE LIKELY HEARD THOSE *super* encouraging (not) statements like:

> "Calm down."
> "Just don't think about it."
> "Stop worrying so much. You know half that stuff never even comes true."
> "You don't look nervous; it can't be that bad."
> "You sure overthink a lot, don't you?"
> "Don't be so dramatic."
> "You are so sensitive."

I could add a list of additional statements that other people tell us when we are on the brink of a freak-out, perhaps because they think that these statements are helpful. But probably not. Since anxiety is a contagious emotion, they probably say these things because it makes *them* feel better in that moment. However, these statements are anything but helpful. If it were that easy to stop feeling the weight of the world on our chest, wouldn't we just say these things to ourselves?

When I'm in the throes of panic, I often wonder how it is not completely obvious to other people that I am about to lose my mind. But the internal process is much more extreme than what is being revealed externally. The symptoms of mental health distress are mostly internal and so much less obvious than if you were walking around with an arm bone sticking out of your body. Can you imagine? People would be calling 911, whisking you off to the emergency department. But with anxiety and panic attacks, the internal belief that you are going to die raging in your head is more of a silent suffering. Most people don't even realize the state of panic you're in. Therefore, they don't know what to say or how to comfort you.

I've been there. I see you. When you're up in the middle of the night, sweating with bone-cold fear, when you're in front of a group presenting a speech, when you're in a public place questioning your every move, when you overthink every action and behavior until you give up all together, or don't even give something a try, I see you. I see you trying to cope with alcohol, drugs, shopping, gambling, sex, food. I see you avoiding something you think will likely take you down. But I've got you. That's right: I've got you and will walk with you, guiding you. All I ask is that you take this first step. I'm here with you, right by your side. Dig down and find the courage to open up to new ideas and understandings. Because guess what? You are the one creating your own anxiety. So, guess what else? You are the only one who can tame it.

According to the Anxiety & Depression Association of America (ADAA), "Anxiety disorders are the most common mental illness in the US, affecting forty million adults (19.1 percent of the population) ages eighteen and older every year."[1] That is the statistic of people who have sought out help. I can't imagine the number of people who suffer in silence.

WHAT IS ANXIETY AND WHAT DOES IT LOOK LIKE?

Anxiety is an emotion. Just like happiness, sadness, jealousy, excitement, boredom. It is a feeling that pops up from time to time. On a small scale, you can feel a little ping in your stomach, a quick, short breath, maybe a tightness in your chest or throat. Involuntarily, you take a deep breath, sometimes not even realizing that your body is taking over to ease the stress, and you peacefully move on.

Other times, the emotion can hit you hard, immediately. It can be triggered by a past event or ignited by a current trauma. Have you ever been awakened out of a deep sleep at three a.m. in full-on panic, not even knowing what hit you? I've been there, too.

---

[1] "Anxiety Disorders - Facts & Statistics," Anxiety & Depression Association of America, updated October 28, 2022, https://adaa. org/understanding-anxiety/facts-statistics.

No matter how it hits—the slow build up, the anticipation, the out-of-nowhere reaction—when anxiety strikes, it gets our attention. Again, it's usually tough to recognize anxiety in someone else. Often, people can look calm on the outside but feel like an electric current is running through the inside of their body. I'm mentioning this because when you feel this level of emotion, it's common to think that people around you see it and get it. What is obvious to you may not be obvious to others, which makes it important to communicate how you are feeling and what you are needing. I think this is also why people don't seek help. They feel they're the only ones who are experiencing this mind-boggling, loss of control.

Anxiety can appear from anticipation or excitement as well. Some of us probably remember waiting for Santa Claus or throwing a surprise party and waiting for the celebrated individual to walk through the door. Which leads me to another idea that sometimes can be shocking to my clients.

Anxiety is an emotion that we need to celebrate as well.

What did I just say? Celebrate a feeling that makes me feel like I'm going to die?

That's right. We will talk about this in Chapter Five.

Try to remember that anxiety is just an emotion, like happiness, anger, jealousy, or trepidation. Although we mostly speak of anxiety as a debilitating ocean of darkness and never-ending depth, it is also one of the body's most accurate ways to warn us to be aware or to take caution.

That's why I'm writing this book. You are not alone. Most of us have likely been there, and it sucks. I want to help you understand the truth about anxiety and, most of all, help you gain the ability to control your anxiety. This is a game-changer in life. Learning to manage the symptoms of anxiety so you can find your freedom and peace instead of living in fear.

I would like to introduce an amazing client of mine, Isabella. (Of course, that is not her actual name, but this is what I will call her).

Isabella is a thirty-four-year-old woman who lives at home with her parents. She entered therapy with me at age twenty-nine. Her initial complaint was that she was not getting along with her family, and she didn't know what to do. As is very typical, the initial reason that people come into therapy is usually not the actual underlying issue, but I was proud of her for reaching out and asking for help. As we soon started uncovering the deeper issues, it was obvious that Isabella suffered from extreme anxiety.

She said that throughout middle school and high school, she was very reserved and kept to herself. She wasn't allowed to have friends over at her house because her parents were introverted and didn't entertain. Isabella did very well in school, but when it came time to choose a college, she didn't trust her ability to venture out on her own and decided it made better sense to live at home and commute to a nearby community college. Her parents were in favor of that. They viewed the world as a very scary place, and they had no hesitation in communicating their beliefs to

Isabella. Of course, as we tend to do, Isabella inherited her parents' belief system that the world was scary, and it was better to just stay close to home. Her father always drove her to school when she was younger, because he believed driving could be very unsafe, another belief system she inherited from her parents.

As you can see, the thought pattern that was being ingrained was Isabella's parents' inability to trust the world or any of the people in it. Isabella had translated that into her parents' inability to trust her, and therefore she never learned to trust herself. She lived in fear.

After completing her bachelor's degree, Isabella settled in at home and found comfort in reading books and helping her parents around the house. By the time she came to see me, she had never held a job, did not drive a car, was extremely passive, did not have any friends, and had never been in any type of romantic relationship.

Her initial complaint entering therapy was being angry at home, but she and I quickly recognized what it really was: a defense mechanism she learned to use because it made her feel more powerful and in control, but just for a moment. Underneath the anger was extreme fear. She recognized that she suffered from social anxiety, obsessive-compulsive thoughts and behavior, panic attacks, and extreme levels of stress. Isabella had been silently struggling with her fears because she had never opened up to anyone about her internal torment.

After utilizing cognitive behavioral therapy and a medication-management routine, Isabella has learned to take control over her life. She realized that she'd been avoiding her symptoms of anxiety, which made her life much worse. She took steps to face the issues that were overwhelming in her life.

I share this story with you to give you hope. To let you know that there are ways to treat anxiety, and some people do not need to utilize medication to do it. I will teach you a method that I have found successful with thousands of clients I have worked with over the twenty-five years I have been in private practice. I will teach you to look beyond the situation causing the anxiety, and instead, learn to manage your symptoms. So, stick with me, and let's get into the bones that make up anxiety.

TYPES OF ANXIETY

Let's take a minute to understand a little more about anxiety.

If I were to ask you, "Have you ever experienced anxiety?", you may pause for a moment, recall specific situations and remember specific body reactions, and reply, "Yes, I sure have." But if we were all sitting in a room together, around one huge table, describing our experience with anxiety, we may each have a different story.

There are many ways anxiety is manifested. At the time I'm writing this book at the end of 2023, there are currently eleven types of anxiety the Diagnostic and Statistical Manual of Mental Disorders, Fifth Edition[2] acknowledges:

- Anxiety disorder due to another medical condition
- Agoraphobia
- Generalized anxiety disorder
- Panic disorder
- Selective mutism
- Separation anxiety disorder
- Social anxiety disorder
- Specific phobia
- Substance/medication-induced anxiety disorder
- Other specified anxiety disorder
- Unspecified anxiety disorder

As you can see, anxiety manifests itself in a variety of ways, so much depending on the individual's situation, trauma, and chemical makeup. Basically, anxiety is influenced by both nature and nurture factors, our genetics coming into the world, and our exposure to the world throughout our lives.

Anxiety can be secondary or co-occurring to other mental health issues such as but not limited to attention deficit hyperactivity disorder, depression, bipolar disorder, body dysmorphic disorder, eating disorders, fibromyalgia, irritable bowel syndrome, headaches, addiction, and sleep disorders.

---

[2] American Psychiatric Association, Diagnostic and Statistical Manual of Mental Disorders, Fifth Edition (Arlington, VA: American Psychiatric Publishing, 2013), xviii-xix.

Anxiety can manifest differently across various age groups, reflecting the unique challenges faced by individuals at different stages of life. In children, anxiety often presents as frustration, irritability, temper tantrums, and oppositional behavior. They can appear disrespectful, snappy, and express self-deprecating statements. Similarly, adolescents may exhibit these symptoms, but they may also withdraw and isolate themselves, keeping their emotions locked away. It is not uncommon for adolescents to resort to unhealthy coping mechanisms such as alcohol, drugs, or risky sexual behaviors as a means of escape. In adults, these manifestations of anxiety are common as well, accompanied by additional addictive behaviors such as excessive work, compulsive exercise, gambling, or disordered eating.

While these descriptions provide a general understanding of anxiety across age groups, it is important to recognize that everyone's experience may vary based on their unique circumstances and developmental stage. Age and developmental levels significantly influence how anxiety is expressed and experienced. By acknowledging these variations, we gain valuable insights into the complexity of anxiety and its impact on individuals at different points in their lives.

While labeling the many types of anxiety can be helpful if you are conducting a study, when anxiety hits, I really couldn't care less what type it is. I just want it to end.

Self-Reflection #1: Create an Anxiety Scale

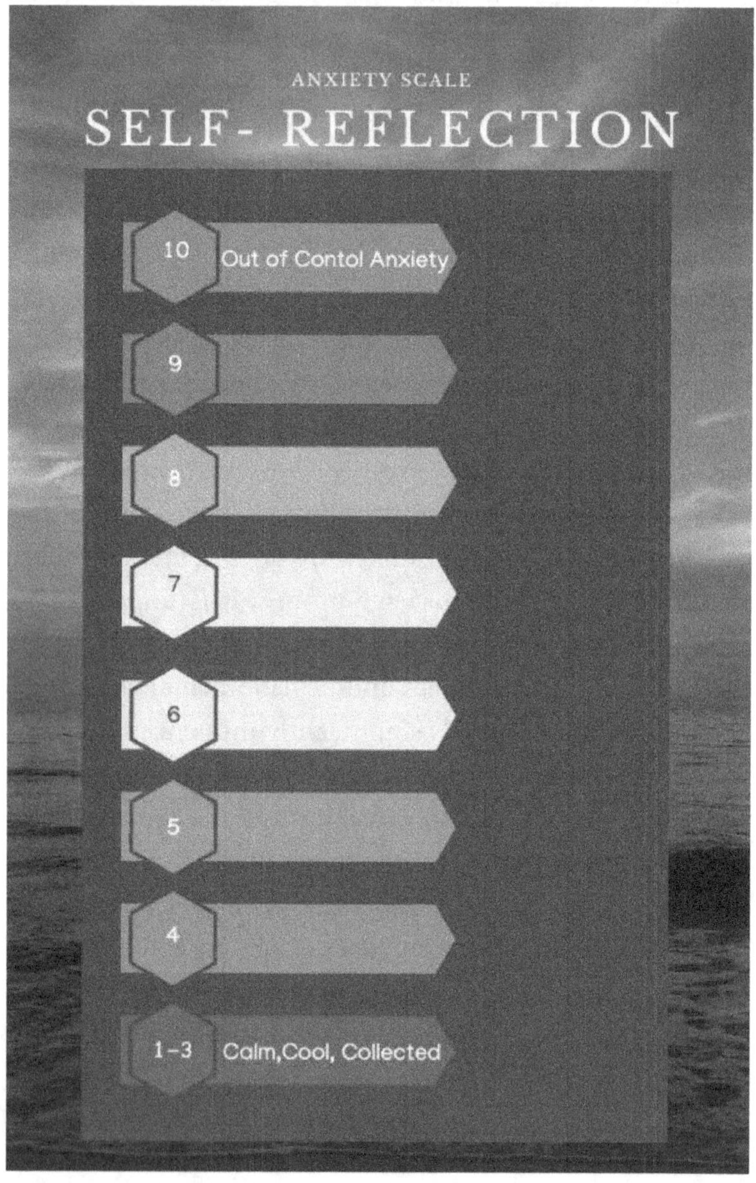

Self-Reflection #1: Create an Anxiety Scale

Your awareness of your anxiety symptoms is crucial if you want to gain control over your emotions. How can you fix something if you don't know what it looks like, what it feels like, and how the symptoms of anxiety manifest inside of you?

Anxiety manifests itself physically, emotionally, mentally, and behaviorally.

In this exercise, you will identify how your anxiety presents itself in its own unique way. Where in your body do you feel it? Is it in your head, chest, stomach, limbs, eyes, or heart? Does it tingle? Does it pulse? Does it ache? Do you experience a shortness of breath? Are you unable to inhale or exhale? Does your mind go blank, or do your thoughts race? Do you lack energy, or do you feel it building like a powder keg inside?

At this time, I'd ask you to grab your journal and turn to a blank page. On the left-hand side of the page, write the numbers one to ten vertically, ten being at the top of the page and one being at the bottom. If you imagine one being completely calm, cool and collected, as if nothing is bothering you and you don't have a care in the world, write down what is going on in your body, in your mind. What is your breath doing? What is your heart rate doing? What and where are your thoughts going?

If you imagine ten being the worst anxiety you have ever felt, like full-on meltdown panic mode, write an example of what is going on in your body at this time: your breath, heart rate, speech, actions; write it all down.

Now fill in the middle. You have the best and the worst. What happens if the anxiety gets turned up just slightly to a two? And a three and so forth. You may assign a color to each number. You may group the numbers together. For example, numbers one to three may represent pretty chill, with a little daily stress. Numbers four to six may represent an uncomfortable tension. Fight, flight, freeze, people please; these are a few common reactions we have, which we will get into shortly. Numbers seven to nine might be severe anxiety, and then ten may feel like a total loss of control.

If creating this list creates some tension, know that you are working toward understanding your symptoms and knowing that as soon as you feel what your one to three look like, that is the first step in applying the coping skills to fully calm yourself. Also, don't forget you are on Chapter One, so cut yourself some slack. This is the beginning of your journey!

Now, you have just created your anxiety scale, based on your unique reactions to anxiety. Remember your number five may look different than my number five or anyone else's, and that is okay.

You can modify this scale because the more you learn about your body and mind, the more you will be able to fill in these levels. Gaining awareness of the symptoms of anxiety will help you understand how and when to insert the coping mechanisms. Keep this scale handy, because we will come back and continue to fill in the coping mechanisms.

IS THIS ANXIETY OR JUST MY CRAZY LIFE?

My clients often ask me, "What is the difference between stress, anxiety, and panic? If I have stress in my life, do I have a panic disorder or anxiety disorder?" Deciding where you lie on the anxiety spectrum can require an assessment by a licensed mental health professional. It can help when developing a treatment plan and when considering if medication is appropriate. A very loose suggestion (and this is not a diagnosis of you, since I likely haven't met you) is if you lie within the one to three range on your scale, it is likely stress. Life events that pop you up into a four to six range will probably occur, and you will learn techniques to manage them. Consistently feeling stress in the six to nine or even ten range over a period of weeks or months can take a toll on your body and could be dangerous. Stress that is not dealt with can easily turn into anxiety. Untreated anxiety can turn into panic.

In my clinical experience, anxiety usually doesn't fix itself. Instead, it festers, gets stronger, and comes out in very inconspicuous and sometime bizarre ways that can be confusing to you. At times, anxiety can be obvious—a tornado near your home causes anxiety. But sometimes, you can be peacefully enjoying a cup of tea, watching the Hallmark Channel, and bam, out of nowhere, you feel a pang of worry and fear. This happens because our brain holds memories and emotions in its own little hope chest, under layers of cozy blankets. Unresolved anxiety can be quietly nestled inside, but all it needs is a trigger, and without you even realizing it, smack, anxiety leaps out attempting to ruin your quiet moment. I hope this book will help you learn to deal with the symptoms of anxiety and guide you to take control over your life. I always encourage my readers to take what they learn in my books and then get help from a licensed professional in the field of mental health, so they can individualize their own experiences and treatment.

WHERE ARE THE ROOTS?

Another common question my clients ask me is, "Where does this anxiety come from?" I completely understand wanting to know this, because if you were able to tie it down to an event, you feel it would be so much easier to manage. Sometimes there could have been a memorable situation that happened that you could trace anxiety back to. It would make sense that fear and worry would occur whenever that situation is presented.

However, most of the time, the symptoms of anxiety cannot be traced back to a specific time or place. One reason for this is that by the time we recognize we are anxious, our mind has created layers of imagination feeding the smallest idea or worry. For example, if an event happened at work, and your boss told you were going to head up a meeting and present something to a large group of people, you may experience some stress anticipating this task. Little do you know, your mind is recalling all the events in your life that you may not even remember that center around being a leader, talking in public, and learning something new. As the deadline approaches, stress may turn into anxiety as your mind comes up with all sorts of worst-case scenarios and what-if's. All of a sudden, you dread going to work.

You may emotionally recover all day Saturday from the stress of the previous week. Anxiety may come out at dinner on Sunday evening, and you have no idea why you feel panicky. Is it dinner on Sundays? Is it the steak and broccoli? You rack your brain wondering where the unsettling feelings are coming from. After stretching your thinking, you may realize that you actually dread Monday mornings, and the fears show up early as a little reminder. And there went the weekend.

This book will guide you away from feeling the need to figure out where the anxiety is coming from and instead help you to focus on the *symptoms* of anxiety. This is where you have most of the control.

I'm looking around my desk as I write this, and I see a huge cup of water. I could have anxiety about this water. What if I reach over to grab a pen, hit the water glass, spill water all over my laptop, and lose everything I have been working on? So, is it really the glass of water causing me anxiety, or is it the rabbit hole of what-if's where my mind can take me? What do you think I might have the most control over? My thoughts, yes! And so do you!

Anxiety is simply another emotion, similar to happiness, anger, jealousy, or even trepidation. It's a part of the human emotional landscape. The way we recognize, and handle anxiety has a profound impact on our ability to practice self-care and retain control over our emotions.

LEVELS OF THE PROGRESSION OF ANXIETY

Anxiety will manifest itself in many ways. Fear, excitement, hyperactivity, laughter, tears, dread, and several other expressions. What if you followed the ray of emotions and tried to pinpoint what actually held facts so you could pin it down and deal with it? That can feel impossible because when anxiety strikes, you feel extremely out of control. I want to simplify how anxiety progresses in your body.

The sequence of events:

1. Your body is always talking to you. Think about this. When you are hungry, what does your body communicate to you? Right, your stomach growls and gurgles. What happens when you're tired? You yawn, and your eyes water. How about when you're cold? You get goosebumps, and you shiver. If you can stop and listen to what your body is telling you, you'll feel a greater sense of control.

2. Because the body has given you a sign and gotten your attention, your mind kicks in and wants to make sense of this sensation. Here are its thoughts: "I must be hungry. When was the last time I ate?" "What time is it anyway? After midnight? Where did the time go? I am exhausted!" "Wow, I left the windows open, and it is chilly in here. I'm glad

summer is coming to an end." (If your brain is like mine, it is very chatty up there!)

3. Time for action. After the body gives the sign, the mind draws a conclusion about the sign, and the brain signals the body to do something and fix whatever is going on: you eat a snack, you go to bed, or you grab a jacket.

Anxiety is no different. The body gives you a sign, the mind creates meaning, and together, they formulate a plan to take action. But it's not always as easy as grabbing a snack. What happened?

The mind has two directions it can go. One is focused on facts, analytics, and strategy. The other is based on emotion and creativity. If the mind is unchecked and undisciplined, it has the ability to create volumes of the scariest horror movie imaginable. The worst case scenarios and the endless "what-ifs" can trick your mind into believing they are reality.

If this happens, the body joins the festivities and creates a surge of adrenaline and cortisol. The mind is being fed more and more of these hormones, which fuels the imagination. Now together, they formulate a plan of how to react. The action they decide is best is to scream, cry, run, lash out, or shut down—basically, a complete meltdown. Here comes the anxiety attack, when in all reality, you were just trying to go to sleep.

The human mind loves drama. Think about this scenario: you want to see a movie at the theater. You show up, pay a million dollars for the movie, your popcorn, and a drink, because movies aren't cheap! You find a comfy seat, sit back, and the lights go down. The film's plot is about a man who lives in a house on a corner of a busy street. He decides to take his dog for a walk. He leashes the dog up, steps out of his house, and starts walking. It's getting dark and cold, but he takes a left, walks down the street, takes another left. It's colder, the wind is picking up, the cars are zooming by. He takes another left and finds his way back home. Finally getting into his warm house, he snuggles up with his dog and falls asleep.

That's it! Lights come on, and your movie is over. Of course you are pissed! You wanted action, drama, chaos. You demand your money back and leave the theater irritated.

Why? Because our brain *loves* drama. It's as if our brain has these little antennas, and they search around just looking to find the juicy dirt, the sappy entertainment. If it doesn't find anything it gets bored. The mind is on a constant hunt for excitement.

Let's return to the person whose boss just dropped the project of giving a speech to a large audience on them. If they have discipline over their mind, they will recognize their body's reactions, gain control over their mind, and allow their body and mind to work together to devise a plan to help them deliver an amazing speech. Without discipline, their monkey mind will go in a million directions, and they will end up having a panic attack.

I am going to teach you how to have discipline over your mind. You will learn to anticipate, not react. (Shout out to my dad. That is his favorite saying and it was ingrained in my brain from childhood!)

Self-Reflection #2: Connecting the Body Reactions to Emotions

Go to your journal where you created the one to ten scale. When you use the sequence of progression of anxiety as discussed above, you can add to your scale using body signs, what the mind begins to create, and then behaviors (reactions) in each section. I like to call each number an opportunity. If you miss what your body is telling you when you feel like you're at a three, just wait a minute, because you are about to escalate to a four. If you miss a meal, your stomach will likely growl loudly in your meeting a few hours later. Are you with me?

You will be able to gain awareness of how anxiety can escalate rather quickly when undisciplined. Continue to fill out your scale based on your symptoms of anxiety. Pay attention to the body feelings, the voice tone and presentation, and the behaviors that continue to intensify as you climb the scale. Each missed opportunity to apply a coping mechanism, which we will talk about heavily in Chapter Four, will allow for the anxiety to increase.

FOUR RESPONSES PEOPLE HAVE TO ANXIETY

Our brain is an amazing mechanism and usually works to protect us twenty-four seven. Like clockwork, when we need to react to pleasure, pain, fear, happiness, our brain enters the room and says, "I'm here and will tell you exactly what to do!"

Most of the time, this is helpful, but when anxiety hits, the communication from the brain to our conscious self can become overwhelming and challenging to navigate. The following are four responses the conscious mind and body work together to respond to anxiety laden situations.

1. Fight—Throwing the claws up, defending yourself to the end, or aggressively attacking someone or something physically, verbally, or emotionally.
2. Flight—An overwhelming urge to escape or avoid a perceived threat. It is usually paired with increased heart rate and shallow breathing.
3. Freeze—This can look like shutting down emotionally, withdrawing from the conversations, or even the situation itself. It may feel as if your mind is going blank, and you're unable to respond.
4. People please—This is also referred to as fawning. The idea is that if someone can just make everyone happy, the tension will release, anxiety will pass, and everything will be okay. While compromise is a healthy conflict-resolution skill, constantly people pleasing leads to decreased confidence. When confidence is low, anxiety increases. This happens because you start to second guess yourself. Not trusting your thoughts and feelings makes you uneasy, and you may find yourself in an unhealthy

loop. To dig into why you may people please or suffer from decreased confidence, check out my book *Preparing for the Jungle: Avoiding Snakes and Pitfalls on the Path to Healthy Love*.

Self-Reflection #3: Assigning Your Unique Reaction to Anxiety

1. Grab your journal and set the timer for two minutes.
2. Begin to brainstorm and write down things that cause you stress, anxiety, or panic.
3. If you begin to become very uncomfortable, stop writing, take some deep breaths, and move onto the next step, even if the two minutes aren't up.
4. Go back and assign a number using the one to four example from above, regarding the way you responded to these experiences you wrote down: one=fight, two=flight, three=freeze, four=people please.
5. Examine if the way you responded was beneficial, or did it result in more anxiety?
6. Do you see a pattern in how you respond to anxiety?
7. What would you like to change? What would you like to keep the same?
8. You may also want to assign a number to the events that cause you stress, anxiety, or panic using the scale one to ten.
9. What did you do to gain control?
10. Make sure you are maintaining a sense of here and now while you do this exercise, and if you become

uncomfortable, put your pen down, take some breaths, and remind yourself you are safe and calm. You can also go to Chapter Four to learn about coping skills. Or you can use the next self-reflection exercise.

Self-Reflection #4: Finding your Calm

Time to chill! I know I just led you through a possibly stress-provoking exercise, and now I want to bring you down to a place of calm and peace.

1. Please find a comfortable and quiet place to sit.
2. If you breathe through your nose and take a big inhale, what is the temperature of the air you breathe in? It is likely cold.
3. Now, exhale the air from your nose and pay attention to the temperature. What do you find? It is likely warm.
4. Next, I want you to either close your eyes, or just look to the floor just past the end of your nose. Breathe in, saying, "cool" and exhale, saying, "warm." Cool, warm, cool, warm, cool, warm.
5. As thoughts come in, say hello to them, put them on a shelf and return to your breath, repeating cool, warm, cool, warm.

I love this exercise, and it usually helps me feel grounded and calm. I hope you will like it, too.

CHAPTER TWO

AWAKENING AND AWARENESS – BECOMING EMPOWERED

LET ME TAKE YOU on a captivating journey into the lives of three of my remarkable clients—Adam, Olivia, and Emily—each grappling with a formidable adversary: anxiety. This invisible specter has wreaked havoc, obstructing their path to sleeping soundly at night, embracing the beauty of travel, and seizing fresh job prospects by tangling them in a web of loneliness and despair.

Now, as I unravel their stories, I challenge you to identify the common thread that binds these three lives together.

Adam is a thirty-five-year-old married father of two. He came to me for help because he was experiencing panic attacks in the daytime as well as in the middle of the night. Adam did not use drugs or alcohol, lived a simplistic lifestyle, and felt fulfilled in his marriage and his job. He was lost as to why he was experiencing these debilitating moments when he thought he would die. After a thorough assessment and ruling out several possible contributors, we discovered two consistent factors: overthinking and lack of deep, restful sleep.

When Adam felt physical pain in his stomach, head, or muscles, he found he would overthink the possibilities of what might be occurring in his body. Because his job was demanding, these thoughts would often occur when he lay down to sleep. The more active his imagination, the harder it was to fall asleep. The less he slept, the more overwhelmed he'd feel in the day, and the more stomach and head pain he would have.

We uncovered that this cyclical process had only worsened over the last few months, leading Adam to reach out for help. In summary, when Adam experienced any medical issues in his body, his mind would race about all the unknown possibilities causing the pain. This would severely disrupt his sleep, and he'd be exhausted the following day; his cycle would start all over again. We also made the connection between his father's death, his extreme pressure to provide for his family physically and emotionally, and his pride in being the sole bread winner.

Olivia, a forty-six-year-old single woman, was once passionate about traveling. She explored numerous destinations worldwide, forging lasting connections with fascinating people along the way. Olivia found fulfillment in her tech-industry job because it fueled her love for travel and enabled her to financially support her adventures. Without warning, Olivia began to worry about her safety when flying in an airplane. On one trip, she experienced some turbulence, but she didn't report that it felt life-threatening at the time. Ever since that trip, she reported feeling extremely anxious at the mere idea of travel. Although she hasn't avoided flying altogether, she has developed a rigid process and routine, that (if not followed with perfection) will cause her to abort the trip and replan for another time.

Olivia has missed out on family vacations, weddings of the friends she met around the world, and many other once-in-a-lifetime, never-to-be-experienced-again events. She entered therapy with me to try and understand how to manage this anxiety that was causing her depression. Travel was her happy place, and her trips took a serious decline. In processing further, we discovered that her anxiety wasn't just in flight, but at work, in meetings, and when conducting trainings. Olivia had learned to "manage" these situations but never dealt with them. Her coping skill to deal with the work stress was to plan a trip, but now, even that was causing her anxiety. The nervous emotion was creeping into every aspect of her life.

In therapy, she realized that anxiety never disappears. Instead, it manifests itself in other situations. She was determined to dig into the roots of her anxiety. This is where we uncovered Olivia's intense perfectionistic and obsessive-compulsive behavior. She identified a developed idea that if she could be perfect in every aspect of her life, people would see her worth, and she could feel internal peace.

Emily is a forty-two-year-old married mom of two kids. She was somewhat fulfilled in her life as a teacher, but she and her husband decided that when they had children, Emily would stay at home. She didn't love her job and was in full agreement to be home and raise her kids. All was fine until the kids went into middle school and high school, and Emily began to experience a low level of anxiety. The kids got involved in their own sports and activities, her husband traveled, and all she could hear in her head was her parents' voices about Emily not living up to her potential and throwing her life away. Emily began to isolate herself from friends, imagining they didn't like her and thought she was dumb and boring. She would try to begin a hobby, but with driving the kids around, keeping the bills organized, and getting the laundry done, she found she never had enough time to fulfill her commitments to hobbies and gave them up. She became very depressed and felt that she had no purpose in life. Her internal dialogue was negative to the point where she just knew people talked about her behind her back, and she feared her husband was having an affair. The sadder she got, the more anxiety she experienced, which fed into depression, another cyclical pattern that anxiety creates.

Emily entered therapy with me to unravel the mess she felt she created and to keep her husband from leaving her. We uncovered patterns in childhood, including very strict parents who believed that no feedback was good feedback, but who wouldn't hesitate to let Emily know when they were disappointed in her. Her parents used critical tactics as their parenting style. We learned how Emily learned to second guess her intuition as a child, and this carried over into her adult life, her marriage, her connection with friends, and her role as a mother. She said her confidence had rapidly declined, and she no longer saw a purpose in life. Emily experienced suicidal ideation when the depression took over any hope she thought she had. In therapy, she learned that her thought process was overtaken by worst-case scenarios. To try to make sense of her thoughts, she would create a story in her head about how horribly she was failing, that her friends didn't like her, her husband no longer wanted to be with her, and her kids had lost respect for her. She also had an eye-opening experience when she realized there was no real proof of any of these things.

THE COMMON THREAD

What is the common thread?

Fear: fear of rejection and fear of abandonment.

Adam was afraid he would become medically compromised, and his wife would take the kids and leave him. He was grieving the loss of his father and watched what his death did to the family.

Olivia had a fear of failure and developed a perfectionistic mindset that led to rigid and obsessive-compulsive behavior. She feared that if she lost control of her life, if things were not perfect, people would doubt her, and she would be alone. Flying in an aircraft was one area of her life where she had zero control, so her panic attacks manifested in the air.

Emily had a fear of her life changing. She was getting older, her kids had found interests of their own that didn't include her, and her marriage was decades old. Emily lost a purpose in her life, her confidence crashed, and she personalized the behavior of everyone around her. The anxiety led to depression, and Emily was afraid of being alone and of her family leaving her.

While fear is a normal emotion, unchecked fear can lead to a person spiraling out of control. Adam, Olivia and Emily's individual situations were all very different, but fear was the base emotion. From there, the anxiety manifested in different ways.

They all entered therapy to understand what had come along and disrupted their lives in such a drastic manner. They talked about the type of anxiety that snuck up on them, attacked them, and then disappeared into the darkness, leaving them with sheer confusion—and fear. Fear of this all-consuming emotion returning and wreaking more havoc.

If fear is the outcome of anxiety, what creates anxiety?

In this chapter, we'll delve into the essence of anxiety, exploring the internal and external factors that give rise to it. We'll also uncover how and why anxiety can influence your life, along with the consequences it carries if left unaddressed.

Let me simplify this. There are two main aspects that create anxiety:

1. Not having a sense of control over your immediate environment
2. The cognitive thoughts of what-if and the creation of fantasy thinking—the creation of the worst-case scenario

LACK OF CONTROL

Let's start with the first aspect of control. If you do a word count about how many times I use the word "control" in this book, you could stack it up from here to the moon. Why? Because not having control, if unchecked, will cause anxiety all day long.

We all need a sense of control in our lives. This doesn't mean we have to be controlling people. It just means we want to know what event is lurking around the corner. We need to plan and anticipate. This helps us relax a little.

A loss of control isn't only about what is to come in the future. We can also feel a loss of control thinking back to past events. Mistakes we have made, or awful events that have happened. We can't act like these things never happened, and we will never forget the memory. Anxiety occurs with past events because we replay them over and over in our minds. Have you ever done this? Apparently, my brain's favorite place to do this is in the shower. There I am, washing my hair, and here come the conversations, replaying what was said, what would have been said if I were in the same situation. *He said this, I said that, they said this.* It's enough blah-blah to make me dizzy.

Do you have control of what will be? No. Do you have control to change what was? No. How much time do you spend wasting energy over trying to gain control over something you can't change or predict? It's exhausting. When you find yourself spinning in the future or the past, you will likely experience anxiety.

COGNITIVE THOUGHTS OF FEAR

The second aspect that creates anxiety is when the cognitive thought process is undisciplined. Cognition is the brain developing ideas or putting meaning to situations. It's what helps us process situations. If you smell delicious pumpkin bread baking in the oven, your mind probably creates thoughts like *Ooh, yummy. That smells great! I'm so glad it's fall. I love Thanksgiving.* And then you may go have a slice of that warm, gooey pumpkin bread.

I encourage you to become familiar with this process because it will help when the cognitive thought process begins to create unsettling ideas. As with the pumpkin bread example, the body experienced a sensation; in this case, a smell. The mind was activated by the body and created an idea of a lovely, fall, Thanksgiving experience. Then there was a behavior or reaction: *I'm going to eat that bread.* Body sensation, thought, behavior.

When the situation presents a disruption, something unpredictable, scary, or unsettling, what does your mind do?

The brain is there to protect you. That is its job, and it will always show up when called on. It will problem solve.

It will run through every possibility like flying through the alphabet and number sequence to create the correct code to unlock a safe full of gold. You can be grateful for your brain when it cracks the code, and a pleasant feeling follows, but what is the feeling when the mind spins out of control? Terror.

The cognitive process of the mind begins with one statement: What-if?.

Okay, you think, *that's all right. I can manage a couple of what-if ideas.* Remember the exercise you did in Chapter One, the scale from one to ten? A few what-if ideas will likely keep you at a two or three.

But the mind loves drama. The mind loves creative chaos; it searches for it. Remember the antennas I talked about in Chapter One? The mind will take one what-if thought and build on it again and again and again.

I visualize this process as wild horses. The calm, majestic animals lay quietly in a field, but there is a fence that keeps them from being able to roam and run. Their instinct is to open the gates to the area where they are contained. What do you imagine happens? Yes, they gallop frantically, to the east, to the west, the north, the south. They are no longer captive, and now that the gate has flung open, they go crazy without direction.

See the parallel?

If you don't stay disciplined in your cognitive mind, a few what-if's can instantly turn into sheer and utter disaster in your mind. Because the brain is always there to protect, it takes over and prepares the body for a worst-case scenario situation, releases the hormones to fight, flight, freeze, or people please, and there you are, in a terrifying panic attack.

But guess what? Whose thoughts are these? Whose brain is this? Yours! So, guess who actually has the ability to control the cognitive thoughts and gain a sense of control over their lives? You!

As a reminder, my goal is to equip you with tools for managing anxiety, and we'll repeatedly delve into an array of these tools. Ultimately, you must learn to manage the symptoms of anxiety. Managing the symptoms is imperative to gaining a sense of control over your life. Let me repeat that. Managing the symptoms is imperative to gaining a sense of control over your life.

INTERNAL AND EXTERNAL FACTORS TO BE AWARE OF

The million-dollar question remains. What causes anxiety? Where does it come from? The answer that is worth next to nothing is…it's complicated. Not exactly what you wanted to hear, but let me help dissect this.

Although feeling a sense of losing control and having the mind race with thoughts based in the space of the unknown is the result, I want to continue to peel the onion layer with you. Because we have unique backgrounds, experiences, genetics, and personalities (to name a few things that make us all individually amazing), here is where

I will challenge you to understand what lies deep inside your psyche.

There are internal and external factors that influence how we react to our environment, and in this next section, you will have a chance to reflect on what pertains specifically to you.

Decades ago, I went on a cruise with my family. We got to the part of the cruise where they took us to a private little island, so we could get in the ocean, relax in the sand, and just take in all the beauty of that salty air. So, of course, we did just that.

I was curious about what lived under the line of vision between the blue sky and the depths of water that stretched as far as I could see. As much as I fought the fear of getting eaten by a shark, I found myself out in the waves.

All of a sudden, we heard the thundering sound of a horn over and over again. Naturally, I panicked, thinking a shark was headed straight for my toes, and I swam as fast as I could toward shore. You know that feeling you can create in your body, the way you can feel getting bitten, almost like a sinking pain in your core? Well, I had that. But as I got safely to the shore, I was quickly relieved that it wasn't a shark attack warning horn, but the cruise staff alerting us to a shift in the weather. Oh, just the weather. Huge relief.

We lined up as the smaller dinghy boats transported dozens of passengers at a time out to the cruise ship. It was our turn to climb onto the petite vessel that would sail us to the safety of the massive ship. On our way toward the cruise ship, the wind picked up rapidly, and the waves started gaining height, which resulted in water crashing into our little boat. We were rocking and rolling like a ride at Disneyland. My impression was how fun that was. The tip of the boat would rise so high that I lost sight of the chopping waves, and then, bam, the boat would slam into the water as our stomachs dropped like lead—again and again. I got out my camera and started taking pictures, laughing, and loving the excitement. I couldn't tell the difference between the rain on my face and the ocean waves splashing off the boat.

However, as I looked around at the other passengers on our little dinghy, I saw that some were terrified. One passenger threw up. Suddenly, I had to reorganize my thinking. Maybe we were actually in danger. Their anxiety was contagious, and it was landing on me. When we made it to the ship, the United States Coast Guard people were tethered to the ship so they wouldn't blow away in the hurricane-like winds. They would take our hands to pull us off the dinghy and onto the cruise ship. It was then I realized the storm had blown in incredibly fast, and we were lucky to safely get to the ship in time.

This is an example of many aspects. First, let's compare me to the gentleman who vomited on the boat (sorry for the visual again; it was very gross, but that's what happened to the poor guy). My personality is one who seeks adventure, loves thrills and excitement. My past didn't exist of trauma in the water or on a boat. My upbringing was not that of avoiding the unknown. In fact, I was encouraged to explore. Although I never got to know my queasy passenger friend, he may have had a very reserved, take-no-risks, trauma-of-storms kind of past.

I just want to point out that this is why it's hard to answer that million-dollar question of what causes anxiety. You must understand yourself to understand and possibly predict what can cause your anxiety.

WHAT ARE INTERNAL FACTORS?

Internal factors are what make you unique. Here are a few things to consider when determining your list that could lead to symptoms of anxiety:

- Patterns and habits you were role-modeled or developed in your life up to this point; being controlling or go-with-the-flow; being pessimistic, realistic, or optimistic.
- What is your internal dialogue—that voice so easily followed in your mind? Is it encouraging and positive? Is it a drill sergeant?
- Are your hormones in balance, or do they fluctuate? If they fluctuate, how aggressively?
- What memories have made such an impact on your perspective of life, and do these memories have control over you, or do you have control over them?
- What is the quality of your sleep? Too much? Too little? Interrupted?
- What are some somatic reactions in your body that can trigger anxiety? For example, hair standing up on the back of your neck, having a lump in your

throat, tingly fingers and toes, that zinger that hits you in the stomach?

WHAT ARE EXTERNAL FACTORS?

External factors are stimuli that occur around us, but based on our uniqueness, we interpret them differently and, therefore, have a different emotional reaction. For example, I am a ravenous gum chewer. I chomp, I blow bubbles, I pop my gum. My sister-in-law has a visceral reaction when she sees or hears anyone chewing. Her external factor that makes her go bonkers is when I chew my gum around her. I, however, do not share that experience. Here are some external factors to consider when you make your list of external factors that could trigger anxiety for you:

- Gum chewing
- Balls bouncing
- Informational overload: too much social media, too much watching news
- Substances such as alcohol, marijuana, or any illegal or prescription drug
- The environment: too hot and humid, too cold and windy
- Clutter
- Dogs barking or babies crying
- Noisy or busy working environment
- Past traumas
- Family

- Other people's expectations of you
- Deadlines or being on a time crunch

DEFENSE MECHANISMS

Human beings are the most amazing creatures ever, in my opinion. We are adaptable and resilient. Our defense mechanisms make this possible, but, like anything, too much of a good thing can easily become bad. I wanted to list a handful of defense mechanisms here, but delving into this could be a whole new book. I am listing these for you to identify, in your uniqueness, what defense mechanisms you tend to gravitate toward. In knowing this, you can decide if your defense mechanisms are actually causing you more anxiety, or if they are truly helping you.

- Denial
- Repression
- Projection
- Reaction Formation
- Displacement
- Fantasy
- Identification
- Rationalization
- Sublimation
- Humor
- Anticipation

CONSEQUENCES OF UNADDRESSED AND UNMANAGED ANXIETY ON YOUR LIFE

I reiterate this to my clients frequently: anxiety is a relentless emotion, refusing to mend itself. It might momentarily fade, but it's lurking in the shadows, biding its time with hidden fangs. And then, when you least anticipate it, anxiety will pounce, jaws snapping shut. The unexpected arrival of anxiety is seldom solely about the immediate circumstance: it's a manifestation of the multitude of worries and fears left unaddressed and unleashed. Brace yourself for the dramatic entrance of anxiety—it's a force to be reckoned with.

Neglecting to confront and navigate anxiety, and choosing instead to suppress or deny its presence, can have far-reaching consequences in various aspects of your life. Below is a rundown of areas that may fall victim to the disruptive influence of untreated anxiety.

- Romantic relationships
- Family relationships
- Career paths
- Work environments
- The way you parent and role model for your children
- Physical health: prolonged, high-level stress will kill you
- Mental Health: increased depression, decreased confidence

- o If anxiety is internalized, you may experience less sleep, more illness
  - o If anxiety is externalized, you may experience more outrage toward others
- Overall quality of life

But before you send yourself into a full-on panic attack, stay with me. This book is filled with methods and strategies I have used with thousands of clients, as well as in my personal life, and it works! There is a way out, and I am going to teach you all of what has clinically proven positive outcomes. However, I encourage you to take this seriously and get working on what I'm offering you here.

At the time I'm writing this book, I have a private Facebook group called "Overcoming Waves: Anxiety Support and Solutions ." I welcome you to check it out and become part of a community of like-minded people. I provide live education sessions and offer tools and techniques for my group members.

Self-Reflection #1: Control in Perspective

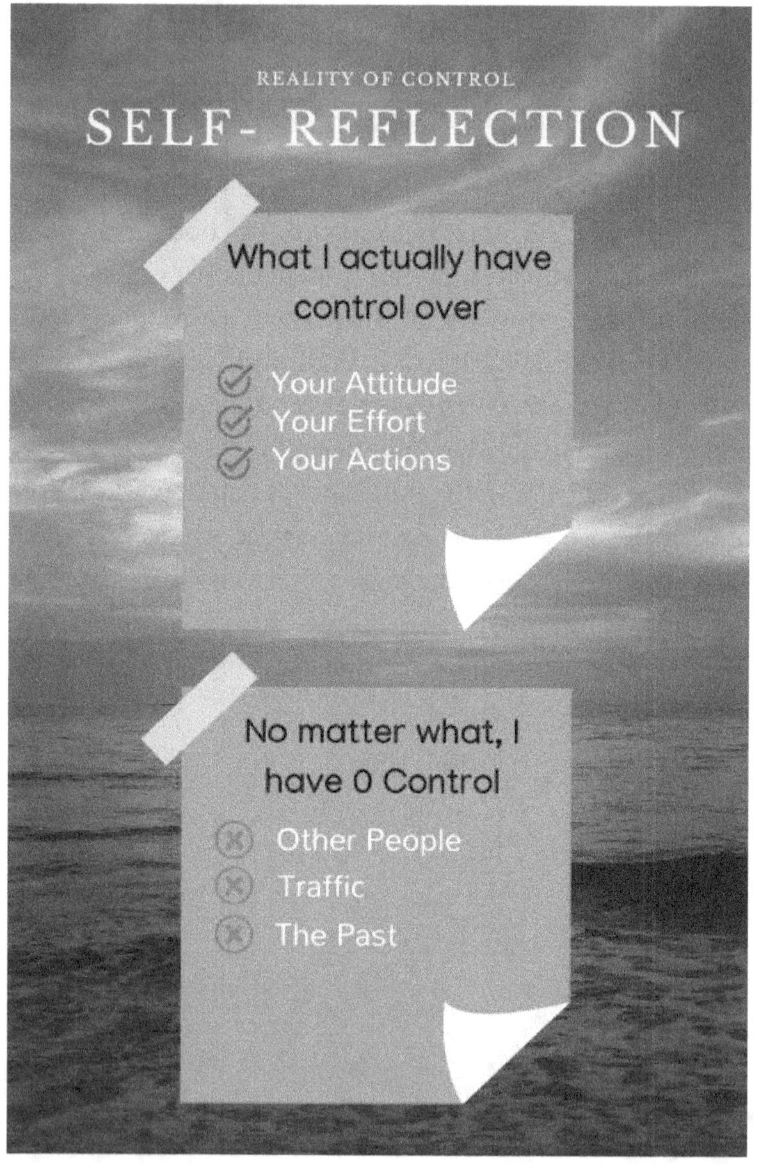

1. Get your journal and go to a blank page. Draw a line down the middle of the page. On the left-hand side, write at the top of the page, "What I actually have control over." On the right-hand side, write at the top of the page, "No matter what, I do not have control over this."

2. Start on the right side of the page and jot down a few ideas that are causing you to feel out of control. Pick two to three aspects.

3. Pick one situation that you wrote down and circle it with a red pen. Now, given that you feel you don't have any control over this situation, I want you to think of ways that you can find a sense of control over this situation. Write these in-control ideas on the left side of the paper.

If any positive aspect came from COVID, it might be the realization that the world can change on a dime. We learned we had the ability to adapt and be flexible to what became our new normal. Let's take the example of COVID for this exercise.

On the left side, write COVID. It was a period that probably made most of us all feel completely out of control: the inability to see loved ones, go to work, or take care of normal basic needs like grocery shopping. And there was the fear that COVID brought on: we wiped our mail down, we left groceries in the garage to get rid of the cooties, and we learned of the tragic stories of lives being lost. We looked at people who sneezed walking their dog on the other side of the street and immediately held our breath in panic that those little particles would track us down like a missile and get us! What a crazy time. So, the situation of COVID goes on the left.

Now, unattended and undisciplined, the situation of COVID could take you down, and it did to many of us. The percentage of people experiencing anxiety dramatically increased over this time.

The goal of this exercise is to shift your thinking. From the out-of-control ideas on the left, start to make a list on the right-hand side of the things that you actually can control about COVID. For example, you can pay attention to valid resources, you can wear a mask, you can order groceries online, you can get a vaccine, you can avoid large group settings. These are just ideas I came up with in a matter of twenty seconds. Keep going. What else can you do that gives you the reassurance that you can find ways to feel and be in control of this one aspect?

When you repeat this exercise using different situations, you will find that the list of items on the left side—what you have control over—should be much longer than the one factor on the right side. What does that tell you? Where you focus your attention is where your cognitive thoughts and body reactions will follow. Like magic, except it's clinically fact-based!

Self-Reflection #2: The Merry-Go-Round

Self-Reflection #2: The Merry-Go-Round

Who remembers the merry-go-round on the playground in elementary school? You know, the death trap of metal that could fling you off if you didn't hold on tightly? Here is your next self-reflection task.

Imagine this: a vibrant merry-go-round symbolizing the twists and turns of life. Now, picture yourself on the outer edges—those aspects beyond your control, spinning faster and faster. Remember the childhood jitter of possibly flying off?

I invite you to grab a pen and draw this merry-go-round. Label the outer edges with aspects of life beyond your control. Take a moment to feel the energy you might be giving to these areas.

Now, let's shift to the center—the calm amidst the whirlwind. Picture yourself there. It's like being a kid on the playground, feeling stable despite the spin.

Back to your drawing. Label the center with aspects you can control. Embrace the stress, but know that in these controllable areas, you're in the driver's seat. Take a moment to reflect on the power you hold in the center of your life's merry-go-round.

I believe in your ability to harness that inner strength. So, go ahead, dive into this reflection task with curiosity and courage.

CHAPTER THREE

CONFIDENCE UNLEASHED – SPARK YOUR INNER FIRE

WELCOME TO THIS DEEP dive into a game-changer: confidence. If anxiety feels like a storm in your mind, think of confidence as your trusty umbrella. Seriously, you won't believe how much it can keep you dry in the downpour of anxious thoughts.

Here's the deal—confidence isn't just a nice-to-have accessory, it's your superhero cape against anxiety's villains. It's time to get real about why boosting your confidence is like giving anxiety a run for its money.

Think of confidence as your personal cheerleader, telling you that, hey, you've got this. We'll break down the nitty-gritty of how confidence acts like a force field, pushing back those anxious vibes. No need for a formal ceremony, just grab a metaphorical cup of coffee, and let's chat about why confidence is your not-so-secret weapon in the battle against anxiety.

We're all about practical stuff here, so get ready for tips, tricks, and a few aha moments. This chapter is like a pep talk for your soul because it's high time you felt confident in kicking anxiety to the curb. Let's get started on this confidence-boosting adventure together!

WHAT DOES CONFIDENCE HAVE TO DO WITH ANXIETY?

The short answer is: everything!

In your mind, visualize a teeter-totter. When your anxiety is high, your confidence is low. When your confidence is high, your anxiety is low. This correlation will present itself in every situation. Think of something you do every day, like brushing your teeth. You are likely a master tooth brusher because you have been doing it several times a day. Do you have anxiety putting the toothpaste on your toothbrush? Do you have anxiety brushing and cleaning out your mouth? No. Why? Because you are confident in this self-care activity. You know how to do it. If your toothpaste plops off your toothbrush, you know exactly how to handle it.

Now visualize a task you have never done in your entire life. For example, if you asked me to stand up in front of a room full of doctorate-level engineers and give a presentation about applied multivariate statistical analysis, I would have a great deal of anxiety because I have no idea what that even is! I would likely start shallow breathing, burst out in cold sweats, and have clammy hands. My voice would shake, and I'd likely just start crying.

Remember in Chapter Two when we talked about not having a sense of control over your surroundings? This example of being completely out of my comfort zone would lead me to feeling anxious and may trigger a panic attack.

See how confidence can directly be related to anxiety? In my first book, *Preparing for the Jungle: Avoiding Snakes and Pitfalls on the Path to Healthy Love*, I aimed to drill in how important strong confidence is when attracting healthy relationships, whether they're romantic or platonic.

My goal now is to share ways you can improve your confidence to gain a better sense of control over your life as well as decrease your anxiety. Topics will include the following:

- Personalizing other people's behavior
- Creating and maintaining healthy boundaries
- Setting short-term, realistic goals
- Communicating effectively
- Trusting your intuition
- Learning how to practice healthy comparing
- Building trust with yourself and others
- Recognizing perfectionism

Whew! This is action-packed, so you'd better grab your journal.

IT'S NOT PERSONAL

Ever find yourself replaying a comment or situation in your head, wondering if you did something wrong? We've probably all been there, and it's like diving into a rabbit hole of self-doubt. We're talking about the art of not taking everything personally.

Whether it's a friend's mood or a random comment, it's time to stop carrying that unnecessary baggage. Trust me, it's not helping anyone, especially not your confidence. Taking things that have nothing to do with you personally can be a confidence killer and a quick way to dial up the anxiety. A little mindset shift can make a big difference.

My client Hilary was twenty-six when she came to me for help with her crippling anxiety. Since as far back as Hilary could remember, she not only fretted over what others might be thinking about her but also took to heart every word spoken and every action taken by those around her. It was like living under a constant microscope, where every external occurrence seemed to be a direct reflection of her actions, creating a persistent sense of responsibility for things beyond her control.

Hilary's tendency to internalize external events took a toll on her well-being and shaped her experiences in profound ways. By shouldering the perceived responsibility for everything around her, she missed out on the freedom to live authentically and without constant self-scrutiny. This habit of personalizing external occurrences created self-doubt, eroding her confidence, and creating a pervasive sense of anxiety.

Hilary spoke of missing the chance to create genuine connections with people. Her growing fear of judgment and the need to constantly prove herself to others left her feeling lonely and isolated.

Moreover, this habit cast a shadow on Hilary's ability to embrace opportunities and take risks. She was so worried about being negatively perceived by others that she felt paralyzed. This prevented her from personal and professional growth. The more she attributed the external events to her own shortcomings, the more she limited her own belief in herself. She became less resilient and confident and turned into a shell of who she really was. This loop of making everything about her created a real anxiety rollercoaster. Self-doubt and anxiety took center stage, drowning out the good aspects of her life like genuine connections and the courage to chase fulfillment.

Imagine carrying the weight of the world on your shoulders when it's not even your load to bear. That was Hilary, stuck in a cycle she needed to break free from. Rediscovering her hidden strength and creating a future without unnecessary baggage became her mission.

Anxiety is like this heavy cloud blocking the sun. Hilary's journey is all about finding that sunshine again.

Ever felt like you needed to let go to find your own light?

Now, the breakthrough moment! Hilary needed to break free from this pattern. It was as if she had this untapped potential waiting to burst out, but she had to let go of the weight first. It was essential for her to rediscover herself and create a future where she wasn't dragging around the baggage of undue responsibility.

It is also time for your breakthrough moment.

Self-Reflection #1: Depersonalizing

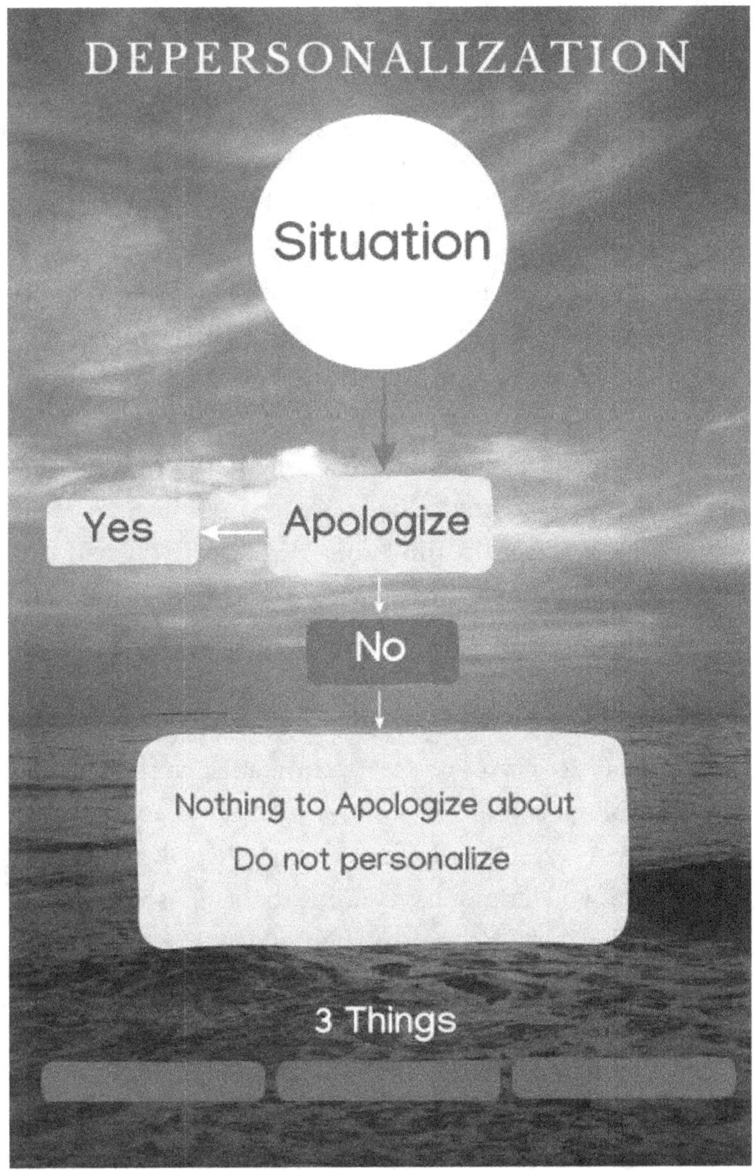

I encouraged Hilary to do this exercise, and I want you to do the same.

1. Identify a situation where you personalize other people's actions, verbiage, or emotions. This is a situation where you do not have actual proof that their "stuff" has anything to do with you, but you have felt a deep sense of dread because your internal dialogue is screaming at you that you probably did something wrong.

2. Got the situation? Got the feeling you likely felt? Good.

3. Now pause the emotional rollercoaster. Ask yourself if you could have done anything to cause this reaction in this other person. If you had this moment to do over again, would you change any of your actions? Could you have possibly caused harm to anyone in this event?

4. If you answered yes to the second question, you need to own up, be accountable, and sincerely apologize.

5. However, if you look back and there was nothing that you could have done to harm someone or make them behave in such a way, I'm here to tell you it likely has absolutely nothing to do with you.

6. Now comes the release of ownership that isn't even yours to carry.

7. Come up with three things that could be going on with that person that have absolutely nothing to do

with you. You won't know these arbitrary issues, but it doesn't matter. You are creating ideas and alternative possibilities as to why this person would have behaved in such a way. You may say, "Why would I come up with fictional ideas, when there is also a fictional idea that I caused their behavior?" Good question. If the idea of you doing something to cause their behavior leads you to feel horrible and yucky inside, yet you have no fact to back it up, why not try an opposite way of thinking? You also have no idea if their behavior *didn't* have anything to do with you, but this way of thinking offers a sense of relief, whereas the other way of thinking will just bring you down. Get it? You are taking control over your unknown thoughts to produce a more positive internal sense of self.

8. If you still need a sense of relief after you have put the effort into managing this situation on your own, you can always go and talk to the other person and ask for clarification. By doing this, you are still taking control of your emotions and promoting healthy communication.

BOUNDARIES, BOUNDARIES, BOUNDARIES

Do you wonder what boundaries, confidence, and anxiety all have in common? Now, we'll explore the essence of boundaries because they will be a pivotal shift in the narrative of your well-being.

Picture boundaries as the trusted guideposts along the winding road of life, providing direction and a sense of security. In this section, we're not unraveling complex theories but diving into the practical wisdom of setting and maintaining boundaries.

You constantly hear advice about setting boundaries, but establishing personal limits is more than a buzzword. Carving out time for yourself while also communicating your needs to others is crucial when strengthening your confidence and decreasing your anxiety.

There are countless types of boundaries you can set for yourself: physical, emotional, verbal, spiritual, monetary, time, and political, to name a few. When you can identify what your boundaries look and feel like, you will be able to set these boundaries with the people around you. You will also find that there is not an all-or-nothing approach to setting boundaries. For example, sharing physical space with someone you despise doesn't mean your boundaries become nonexistent. You can be in the same room but still maintain an emotional, verbal, and mental boundary. You can have a tense political conversation with someone who disagrees with your opinion and maintain a time, spiritual, and emotional boundary.

It is when you feel out of control with your boundaries that anxiety has room to seep in, making you second guess yourself, which will further deteriorate your boundary-setting ability. This can be a vicious cycle. The goal is to have an awareness of your surroundings, establish a comfortable boundary for that specific situation, communicate your needs, and maintain what suits these needs.

Self-Reflection #2: Evaluate Your Boundaries

Grab your journal and use these questions as prompts to gain self-awareness to your unique boundary-setting situation.

1. Where do you struggle with setting boundaries? Do you worry about hurting other people's feelings? Do you worry they won't like you or think you are too pushy or entitled? There is a difference between the two. When you have clearly communicated boundaries and when you are not causing harm to others while being honest with yourself, you are not being too pushy or entitled.

2. Define the different types of boundaries starting with the examples above. Feel free to add more types of boundaries. Are these easy to set and maintain? Which boundary types do you struggle with setting and maintaining? Why is this a struggle?

3. Do you struggle with setting boundaries with certain people? List them and examine the characteristics and meaning of these people in your life. Do you have unresolved issues with them? Maybe it is a person who doesn't respect your boundaries, no matter how kindly you attempt to set them. Is it time to reevaluate these relationships?

Self-Reflection #3: Bullseye

1. Get an unlined piece of paper.
2. Draw a bullseye on the sheet of paper. One dot in the middle and six rings around it.
3. You are the middle dot, the bullseye.
4. The rings around you are your boundaries. They are fluid, not rigid. They indicate the space you need between yourself and people around you.
5. Write names of the people who are in your inner circle. These are people who you fully trust and can be the most vulnerable with. Write names of people on the second ring. These are people who you trust, but not as closely as the people in the first ring. Next, write names of people in the third, fourth, fifth, and sixth rings. Some people come to mind who you'd rather flick off the page, and that is fine, too. This is your bullseye; you can do whatever you want with it!
6. Why did you choose to write these names in these spaces? What is this telling you about your boundaries and which boundaries are the most important to you?
7. Remember the way you organized this is fluid, meaning that just because your wonderful, loving, partner is in the first ring some days doesn't mean you need to scoot them to the second ring at times. All it means is that you are respecting yourself and what you need, honoring you and strengthening your confidence. Watch as anxiety melts the more you grasp setting boundaries.

GOAL SETTING

Ever since you were born, you have utilized goal setting as a method to improve, mark successes, and determine your life course. When you were born, you were given percentages in height, weight, and length, and your mission became to follow a path of growth to indicate the health of your body. It didn't stop there. You were tested in vision, hearing, then crawling, standing and walking. Soon it was about how many words you could speak, how high you could jump, and so on.

Setting measurable goals has been a constant in life, and it is no different when looking at increasing confidence and decreasing anxiety. However, you must know how to set goals because random, impulsive goal setting can lead to feeling out of control, and if you are this far along in this book, you know…feeling out of control is the foundational aspect to anxiety.

The art of goal setting is really pretty simple, but we tend to make it complex by adding all kinds of factors to it, like perfectionism and worrying what other people think, which we'll talk about in a minute. But first, let's simplify.

Self-Reflection #4: Short-Term, Realistic Goal Setting

When setting a goal, I like to start at the finish line and work backward. (I also like to read the last chapter of a novel because I hate surprises, but that's beside the point.)

Starting with the end goal allows you to know when you have successfully completed the mission you are ready to set out on. Let's take the example of running a marathon. If I have a goal of running a marathon, this is my end goal. Could I run a marathon tomorrow? Not a chance in hell, so I know I need to create some time to reach this goal, say, six months. Now, I have the end goal and a rough idea of how much time I should plan. Is this a rigid time frame? No, because rigidity will lead to frustration and doesn't allow room for error, so being flexible in your thinking will promote successful goal setting every time.

I suggest you get another piece of unlined paper, turn it horizontally, and from the bottom lefthand side of the paper, draw stairsteps all the way to the top right side of the paper. Label "End Goal" in the top right corner, at the top of your stair steps. Then at the bottom left corner, write the word "Now". This is your starting point.

I then suggest you brainstorm ideas of what it will take for you to achieve your end goal, then place them in order on your stairsteps. You'll find that you move these items around until you settle on what feels realistic.

These action items in the stairs becomes your short-term goals. The action item at the end of the stairs is your long-term goal. What makes a short-term goal doable? It *must* be short-term because we all need a sense of immediate gratification to keep us motivated and feel that forward progress. They must be realistic; otherwise, we are setting ourselves up for failure.

Remember, just because you don't meet a short-term goal doesn't mean you can't. It just means you have to chunk it down and add a few more shorter-term, more realistic steps. Be flexible in your thinking. I can't stress that enough. Rome wasn't built in a day.

So, back to the marathon example. Say I thought the first place to start was to begin walking two miles every day, and then start jogging. But I realized my shoes were horrible, and my feet hurt. I needed to take a couple steps back, research good running shoes, save up the cash, purchase the shoes, and then I could restart the physical training. Did I throw in the towel because my feet hurt? I could have, but then I would have been so angry, telling myself what a failure I was. No: I took a pause, assessed the situation, pivoted, and rearranged my short-term, realistic goals. Now I am back on the path, physically and figuratively, to work toward the end goal.

Also worthy to note, as I continue my path to run a marathon, I may include yoga into my weekly training program. I may also enjoy yoga so much that I reevaluate my end goal to run a marathon and decide I no longer want to accomplish this. I give myself credit for listening to my mind and body, trash my original stair-stepping sheet of paper, and create a new long-term goal to get certified and teach yoga. (True story, by the way, and it couldn't have been a better fit for me!) If you force yourself into doing something that every fiber of your being is telling you not to do, you compromise your internal sense of self and will likely regret the end goal, not to mention the decrease in your confidence. And—fill in the blank—increase your anxiety.

To recap: setting short-term, realistic goals is the fastest way to improve your confidence and decrease your anxiety. By achieving the smaller steps, you prove to yourself that you have worth, maintain the ability, and celebrate what you work toward. For the most part, you only need to depend on yourself, not on other people to reach your goal, which is ultimately the most empowering feeling ever!

EFFECTIVE COMMUNICATION

If you happened to have read my first book, this next section will be a reminder of how important communication types are, but here, we will focus on why they are important in relation to anxiety.

The four communication types are passive, aggressive, passive-aggressive, and assertive. Three of the four will severely compromise your self-worth, and one will strengthen it.

As humans, we all want to be heard and listened to. When people don't honor this, we feel invisible, worthless, isolated, and unnecessary—obviously, confidence-wrecking emotions. It is easy to look around and blame other people for our feelings of rejection and abandonment; however, sometimes, we are the problem. How we present ourselves and communicate our needs can determine the degree that people want to listen to what we have to say.

Sometimes taking a passive approach is okay, but I will focus on when it no longer serves us in a healthy way; for example, keeping our opinions and needs to ourselves and feeling sad. We don't speak up, or we do so in such a mild manner that no one can hear us. We become too agreeable and people please-y. When we communicate this way, our confidence tanks.

Being aggressive has its healthy place, like in an emergency when being commanding promotes safety. However, communicating with aggression will likely lead to shutting people down, encouraging others to build walls and not want anything to do with us. We then wonder where everyone went, again feeling isolated and rejected. Confidence tanks.

When we communicate in a passive-aggressive style, no one knows what we are talking about. We draw people in, and then figuratively bop them on the head. We want others to get closer to us, but due to a lack of confidence and fear of vulnerability, we push them away. This method can make us feel a loss of internal focus, resulting in a decrease in confidence.

However, the assertive communication style involves being focused, clear, firm in what we want and need from others, but speaking in a compassionate way where people want to know more. People want to listen and hear what our opinions and desires are. They are drawn to be a part of the conversation because, not only are we respecting ourselves with this style, we are also respecting other people, and they reciprocate that. Confidence improves, anxiety decreases.

Self-Reflection #5: Identify Your Communication Style

Journal time. Dedicate a section of your journal to analyzing your typical communication style. Is it helping you feel grounded and clear? Do you feel like people want to take time to understand what you need? If not, identify if you are being too passive, too aggressive, or too passive-aggressive. What can you do to shift this method of delivering your message?

The goal is to be so aware of your communication style that you can anticipate situations involving certain people where it is more difficult to be assertive. Plan ahead, take a pause, and collect your thoughts before you enter into the conversation.

The longer-term goal is to recognize when you are in the middle of a tough conversation where it would be much easier to shut down or get aggressive. Catch yourself, take a quick pause, regroup your thoughts, and proceed with assertion. It takes practice, but you'll save yourself a lot of trouble and heartache. You'll also watch the confidence level multiply with strength.

COMPARE WITH CLASS

I often read quotes and see memes that encourage people to stop comparing themselves to other people. Have you ever honestly tried to not compare yourself to others? I bet you get frustrated after a while because it's impossible! We learned to compare at such a young age and are rewarded for our ability to compare throughout life. Do you feel more comfortable with this group of friends, or that group? Do you like Italian food or Chinese? Do you need to wear a coat today based on the weather from yesterday? Life is all about comparisons.

Comparison comes in both healthy and unhealthy flavors, so, let's dissect the distinction. When you find yourself sizing up against someone whom you perceive as having more or being better, it often acts as a barrier, hindering your capacity to feel good about yourself.

What I mean is we look at other people and think, "Oh, if only I looked like her. If only I drove a car like that guy. I wish I could be successful like her." Inadvertently, you are telling yourself, "You are ugly. You don't deserve to drive that car. You are not successful." When your internal dialogue repeats these statements, you will adopt this thinking. What you think, you believe. And what you believe, you become. Confidence is dwindling.

Self-Reflection #6: Practice Comparing with Class

1. Gain awareness of when you compare yourself to other people. It's going to happen, and it likely happens several times a day. But catch yourself once, and let's analyze it.

2. What is it about this person with whom you are comparing yourself? Looks, the company they keep, the material things they have, the attitude they exude? Really narrow it down and get specific about what you are pitting that they have against what you think you do not.

3. Is this trait something that you honestly want in your life? Are you willing to do the work to achieve whatever it is you are thinking you so desire?

4. If yes, go back to Self-Reflection #5 and create your short-term, realistic goals so you can take control of this situation and put the ownership back on yourself. If you want to achieve the better job, fitter physique, the increased social circle, what do you need to do to make these shifts in your life?

5. However, if you decide that you are happy with the job title you have, the car you drive, the home you live in, the company you keep, evaluate what you are grateful for. Make a list of why you are grateful for these aspects in your life. Then you can look at the other person and be happy for them. You can celebrate the other person. Watch the automatic shift in your body. You went from snipping that person apart in your mind, to having compassion.

Comparing yourself to other people is a habit that's highly encouraged in our culture. All you have to do is look at all the advertising that goes on in the media. We are constantly reminded that we are not good enough and need to spend money on specific products to make our lives better and more fulfilling. We have to fight the automatic response to believe these marketing ads and immediately feel bad about ourselves. It's easy to get brainwashed and make impulsive decisions, yet if we just take a moment and pause, we may realize we are already content and don't need to spend unnecessarily.

To recap, comparing yourself to other people is very normal. If you seem down in the dumps or anxiety ridden after making these comparisons, you are probably comparing in an unhealthy way. Instead, try these ideas and hopefully, you can make that shift, do the natural comparing, and feel at peace internally. Confidence up, anxiety down.

BUILD INTERNAL TRUST

Learning to trust your gut feeling is probably the most important aspect of building confidence. Your internal instinct, the little voice in your head, the existence of your consciousness; it doesn't get any more internal than that, and if you are constantly second guessing this, how do you think your confidence is rating? Likely very low.

In the world of anxiety, it's not uncommon to find folks second-guessing their gut feelings, that inner compass we all have. Sometimes, we do this because of the pressure from society to not set boundaries, to go with the flow, even though your gut is saying no. So we doubt what we think we feel. Other influences are the fear of being judged or the need to fit in, which can mess with what our gut is telling us. This creates a gap between what we feel and what we think we should feel.

This back-and-forth not only clouds our decision-making but also takes a hit on confidence. Trusting your gut is like giving yourself a pat on the back—it's saying, "Hey, I know what's up." But when you start doubting those feelings, it's a confidence drain. The goal becomes about rebuilding trust in ourselves.

Ideas to rebuild trust can be meditation, mindfulness, recalling times in your life when your gut feeling was spot on, and letting go of external pressures that make your heart feel heavy.

I want to offer a tool I use with clients to not only learn to regulate their emotions, but also learn to evaluate their responses to situations, assess if the level of the response matches the level of the situation, and then make the necessary adjustments if there is a mismatch. Let me explain.

Self-Reflection #7: Evaluating the Congruency of Your Reactions

1. Back to the drawing board. Get yourself a piece of unlined paper and turn it horizontally.
2. On the top left-hand side of the paper, write the word "Situation." On the top right side of the paper, write the word "Reaction."
3. I like to get colored markers for this because it helps my brain ingrain the exercise even more. On the left side of the paper under the work "Situation,"

write the word "Red." Under that, write the word "Yellow," and under that, write the word "Green."

4. Repeat this on the right side of the page. Now, you have the words Red across from Red, Yellow across from Yellow and Green across from Green.

5. Next, reflect back to the last week or couple weeks or even the last month. Identify a conflict-filled situation you experienced, jot down some of the facts that you remember about that situation, under the word Situation.

6. Under the word Reaction, write down some of the ways you reacted: physically, mentally, emotionally, behaviorally.

7. Now, rate the situation. Was it a Red—emergency, extremely chaotic, trauma-filled—situation? Was it a Yellow—stressful, caught you off guard, jumbled your head for a minute—situation? Was it a Green—someone out of the ordinary caught your attention, but overall manageable—situation? This is going to be your perception, not your partner, or your best friend, or your neighbor's perception. This is your perception of the situation.

8. Now, rate your reaction in the same way. Did you react Red—hair of fire, Yellow—stressed and heightened but still in control, or Green—cool as a cucumber, thoughts intact?

9. Evaluate your findings. If the colors matched up across the board—that is, a Red situation matched a Red reaction, and so forth—you can remind

yourself that your gut feeling is likely spot on, and you should listen to it. If the situation was Green, and you reacted with Red, or the situation was Red, and you reacted with Green, you may need to evaluate how much you are listening to your intuition and work toward building a better connection with your conscious mind.

Repeated instances where your response doesn't align with your perception of a situation can erode trust in this inner, deeply connected part of yourself. The consequence is a decline in confidence and a surge in anxiety.

PERFECTIONISM VS PRAGMATISM

Ever find yourself stuck in the perfectionism trap? It's like setting the bar impossibly high for everything you do. You end up stressing over every detail, fearing any misstep will lead to failure. Guess what? This perfectionistic thinking is a one-way ticket to higher anxiety levels. It's a never-ending cycle of self-criticism and stress.

Now, enter pragmatism—the laid-back, more realistic cousin to perfectionism. Being pragmatic means setting achievable goals and focusing on progress rather than an unreachable standard. Unlike perfectionism, it's not about obsessing over flawless outcomes. It's about embracing the journey, imperfections, and all. Choosing pragmatism is like giving yourself a break. You'll find less anxiety, more resilience, and a whole lot more room to breathe. The goal is to ditch perfectionism, which usually ends in a sense of failure, and opt for a healthier, pragmatic mindset. It's the key to a less stressed, more balanced life.

Becoming aware of perfectionistic thinking is the first step to changing what does not serve you. In order to gain this awareness, you will have to pay attention to your body. Are you exhausted, overwhelmed, feeling like you can't accomplish anything, and tasks are piling up? Do you feel as if your efforts are never good enough? Do you feel like you constantly let others (but mostly yourself) down? Are you short and snippy with people you love? These self-reflective questions are important to ask and take a minute to honestly answer. For a little more elaborating, follow these journal prompts.

Self-Reflection #8: Perfectly Imperfect

Find your journal and carve out about fifteen to thirty minutes to settle into a quiet space in your mind and body. Here are ten journal prompts to choose as you evaluate a perfectionistic mindset while evaluating how this is damaging your confidence and creating more anxiety.

1. Reflect on a recent situation where you felt the need to be perfect. How did it impact your confidence and stress levels?

2. Consider the standards you set for yourself. Are they realistic, or do they tend to be unattainably high? How does this impact your overall well-being?

3. Explore a moment when you achieved a goal but still felt dissatisfied. What expectations did

you have, and how did they contribute to your dissatisfaction?

4. Think about a time when you made a mistake. How did you react, and what did you learn from the experience?

5. Examine your self-talk. Are you often critical of yourself, even in small moments? How does this influence your confidence?

6. Consider the activities or tasks you avoid due to fear of not doing them perfectly. How does this avoidance affect your personal growth and development?

7. Reflect on the role of external validation in your life. How much does the approval of others contribute to your sense of self-worth?

8. Think about a situation where you were faced with uncertainty. How did your perfectionistic mindset impact your ability to navigate ambiguity?

9. Explore the idea of embracing imperfection. Can you identify a situation where letting go of the need for perfection actually led to a positive outcome?

10. Consider your long-term goals. Are they realistic, or do they contribute to a perpetual cycle of chasing an idealized version of success? How does this impact your overall happiness and fulfillment?

You can also use the following ideas to help remedy a perfectionistic mindset:

1. Reframe Perfection: Instead of aiming for perfection, set achievable goals and acknowledge progress as a success.
2. Set Realistic Standards: Evaluate and adjust the standards you set for yourself to be more attainable and aligned with your capabilities.
3. Celebrate Achievements: Focus on acknowledging and celebrating your accomplishments, no matter how small, rather than dwelling on perceived shortcomings.
4. Learn from Mistakes: Instead of being self-critical, view mistakes as opportunities for growth and learning. Consider what lessons can be gleaned from the experience.
5. Positive Self-Talk: Cultivate a habit of positive self-talk. Replace self-criticism with encouraging and affirming thoughts, especially in challenging moments.
6. Face Avoidance: Identify tasks you've been avoiding due to fear of imperfection. Challenge yourself to tackle them gradually, focusing on the process rather than the outcome.
7. Internal Validation: Shift your focus from external approval to internal validation. Recognize your worth independently of others' opinions.
8. Embrace Uncertainty: Practice embracing uncertainty. Develop coping strategies to navigate ambiguity without succumbing to perfectionistic tendencies.

9. Celebrate Imperfections: Reflect on situations where imperfections led to positive outcomes. Embrace the idea that perfection is not a prerequisite for success.
10. Set Realistic Long-term Goals: Evaluate and adjust your long-term goals to be more realistic and sustainable. Prioritize a fulfilling journey over an idealized destination.

This chapter is purposefully intense because the stakes are equally intense. Please take your time with the tools I've included here. The more you reread and apply what you have reflected upon in your own life, the more confident you will feel. I'm not talking about the confidence that is a quick flash in the pan, but a lasting, authentic new way of living your life. The more grounded and intentional you are in your body, mind, and spirit, the more confident and less anxious you will feel.

CHAPTER FOUR

FROM CHAOS TO CALM – THE SIX-STEP STRATEGY

IN THE TAPESTRY OF my life, anxiety has been a daunting thread. This relentless companion would appear out of nowhere, wearing different masks and of varying intensities, but always leaving its footprint on my inner world. It appeared, wreaked havoc, and then vanished away into the shadows.

These anxious episodes were more than just casual disruptions; they were complex episodes silently battling in my head. The toll these wild rides took on my mental landscape left me toying with a distorted reflection of myself. Anxiety could rearrange the pieces of my identity puzzle, scattering them everywhere. It has a strange power to toss these pieces all over the room, leaving me to figure out the disaster and rebuild a sense of wholeness.

I vividly recall the time when I was a new mom at the age of thirty. I had grappled with anxiety throughout my life, but the arrival of a precious little baby amplified everything, sending my anxiety into overdrive. It was as if a switch had been flipped, and my mind was engulfed in worry.

I found myself in a session with a client, attempting to maintain composure while my anxiety waged war within me. Suddenly, it hit me like a freight train, crashing into my thoughts with relentless force. I couldn't sit still for a moment. With each passing second, the urge to move became more overwhelming.

I kept finding excuses to rise from my chair, pretending to search for something at my desk, only to return to my seat in a futile attempt to regain control of the session. My heart raced, and beads of sweat formed on my brow, while my mouth felt parched, as if I had been stranded in a desert without water.

I was a hot mess. I was mortified by my behavior and reaction to this overwhelming sense of doom that seemingly came out of nowhere. The session finally ended, and there in my office, by myself, I completely lost it.

At that moment, I knew that enough was enough. "I'm a psychotherapist, for Christ's sake," I said to myself. "Get your shit together, Tami!" That is when I flipped into clinician mode as I became determined to figure out a solution to this anxiety thing. I kept telling myself that I am the one creating these anxiety-producing thoughts. Therefore, I am the one who can shift the thinking and calm my mind. I am the owner of my thoughts and feelings, even though anxiety works really hard to make me doubt myself. Sound familiar?

Over the years, I have gathered information and created these self-reflection strategies for you. I'm confident that practicing these will help you ingrain the belief that you too have control over your thoughts and behavior.

I developed the six-step, clinically proven strategy, which, when you follow it, will cause your anxiety to dissipate as you regain your sense of freedom and peace. As I applied this strategy to my own journey, I witnessed its profound impact.

Now, as I share these steps with my clients, I watch their transformation from fear to empowerment, I can't help but feel an urgency to broadcast this revelation from the rooftops. The six-step strategy is not just a roadmap; it's a powerful tool for anyone seeking to take command over their anxiety. I'm excited for you to delve into its effectiveness and experience the liberation it brings to your own journey.

The six steps to follow in order are as follows:

1. Gain awareness
2. Control powerful breath
3. Activate the left brain
4. Apply cognitive discipline
5. Focus on the facts
6. Identify gratitude

STEP 1- GAIN AWARENESS

Anxiety can be terrifying. The surprise element, the powerful punch, the wave of disillusion, the exhaustion following, the scarred confidence. Of course, we want to rush in and fix it, make it disappear, rushing to find a sense of peace. But when we approach anxiety with this mindset, we often make it worse. We can't fix it automatically, which only perpetuates the emotion as it gains more momentum.

Remember in Chapter One, we talked about the importance of awareness as a first step to making changes in your life. You can't change something if you aren't aware it needs fixing.

When anxiety strikes, the first thing to do is *be aware* that the feeling is anxiety, and it is only an emotion.

Being in tune with what your body is telling you is a skill you can strengthen. Here are a few ways to master the art of picking up clues that your body is laying out for you. Practice these methods on a daily basis regardless of whether you are anxious. By doing this on the regular, you will begin building a habit and creating a new baseline for your natural emotional state. The goal is for the baseline to be calm, not always in crisis mode.

- Meditate. Self-guided or guided using a video or app.
- Take a pause three to five times in your day. Check in with your breath, thoughts, muscles, heart. Are you calm? Are you amped up? Are you hungry? Tired? Stressed? Just observe.
- Breathe. Use the techniques we talked about in Chapter Three.
- Check in with your body. Practice body-scan meditation. Lie in a comfortable position. Begin with

your feet. Inhale and scrunch up your toes, exhale and release your toes. Inhale, scrunch up your calves, exhale and release. Go through each body part all the way to your head and face. Inhale as you tighten, exhale as you release. Complete the exercise inhaling and tightening up your entire body, then exhale and relax everything. Nighty night!

- Journal. Write about your day, your feelings, your emotions, anything. Just write. It helps get what is stuck in your head out onto paper.

- Practice yoga. Even a ten-minute body stretch break can make a difference in a busy day.

- Identify areas of your life that can pile up and weigh you down. When you avoid these aspects, they just get louder in the back of your mind. Jot them down to acknowledge them and maybe even identify a starting point to manage.

When you can become more in touch with what your body is trying to tell you, you'll be able to identify the early signs of anxiety. Catching these signs when they are more manageable will help you avoid increased anxiety symptoms.

Although it is difficult to put these practices into place when a wave of anxiety strikes, sometimes just being aware that you are experiencing anxiety can help label what the emotion is. Often people feel the panicky feeling and jump to fearing a heart attack or death. That isn't helpful when it's only your nervous system firing up.

STEP 2- CONTROL POWERFUL BREATH

The second step when anxiety strikes is to become aware of your breath. Your ability to breathe is magic. Not only does your breath support your life force, but it is directly connected to your nervous system. The breath sends signals to the nervous system commands it to speed up or to slow down; to become more active or to take rest.

There are two parts to the autonomic nervous system, the sympathetic and the parasympathetic.

When you take short, shallow breaths from the top part of the lungs and from the chest only, your breath is communicating a message to the sympathetic nervous system to become active. Your sympathetic nervous system responds, calls all the troops to the rescue, releases cortisol and adrenaline, to prepare you to react and protect. Following are some of the fascinating responses from the body when the sympathetic nervous system is activated by a perceived or real threat.

- Increased heart rate
- Dilated pupils to allow more light in so you can see better
- Increased blood pressure
- Muscles contracted and prepared for action
- Liquid retained by body—urine is secreted while mucus and saliva dry up

However, when you take long, deep breaths from the lower abdomen all the way to the top of the lungs, your breath is communicating a message to the parasympathetic nervous system to calm down: it's urging your body to relax. Some responses you will notice when the parasympathetic nervous system activates are the following:

- Heart rate and blood pressure decrease
- Pupils constrict
- Saliva, mucus and urine secretion increases
- The large and small intestines regain activity and mobility

The breath is powerful, but only if you use it with intention. In this case, you want to calm your body, so slow, deep, controlled breath is crucial.

Self-Reflection #1: Breath and Heart Rate

Find your pulse on your wrist or your neck. Got it? Feel the pulse and become aware of the speed. As you inhale, what does your pulse do? If you said, "It speeds up when I inhale," you are correct. Now, what does your pulse do when you exhale? If you said, "It slows down," you are correct. What does this tell you about your breath? It controls the speed of your heart rate. Because we want to activate the parasympathetic nervous system, and we want our heart rate and blood pressure to decrease, this next breathing technique is just what we need.

1. Inhale slowly and deeply and count to three.
2. Pause.
3. Exhale slowly and count to five on the way out.

a. The inhalation is less counts than the exhalation because we want to use the exhalation to slow everything down.

4. Now try to inhale for the count of five and exhale for the count of seven.

5. Can you try an inhale for seven and an exhale for nine?

6. Try this three times in a row and tell me you don't feel like taking a nap.

(Self-disclosure: when I am at the doctor's office and they take my blood pressure, I use this technique to see how low I can get the number. I'm competitive like that. Yes, even when I am trying to calm down. Hence, my own anxiety.)

Self-Reflection #2: Box Breathing

Box breathing is a common coping technique to find calm and peace. It is like the technique in Self-Reflection #1, but you visually and mentally trace a box.

1. Inhale as you mentally draw a line going up; this is the side of the box.

2. Pause at the top.

3. Exhale as you mentally draw a line across.

4. Pause at the corner.

5. Inhale as you mentally draw a line going down.

6. Pause.

7. Exhale as you draw a line at the bottom to close the box.

8. Pause and repeat.

Self-Reflection #3: Temperature Focused Breath

Remember this technique from Chapter One? Now is the time to implement it in the six-step series. Close your eyes. When you breathe in through your nose, say, "Cool." Now, exhale slowly through your nose and say, "Warm." Sit and just tell yourself on the inhale, "Cool," and tell yourself on the exhale, "Warm." Over and over, cool, warm, cool, warm.

I use this technique when I am anxious, and it works. Here's why: one, you are breathing slower and deeper when you are aware of the temperature, and two, you are utilizing a different part of your brain to determine if the air is cool or warm. We will talk about this in step 4, but because you are shifting the thinking from the anxiety provoking though to identifying the temperature of your breath, you will feel a sense of calm wash over you.

Any breathing technique you conduct with the intention to calm down is helpful, *intention* being the key word.

STEP 3- ACTIVATE THE LEFT BRAIN

Now you have become aware of the emotion you are experiencing; you've used intention to calm and slow the breath. It is time for my favorite part of the six-step model to decrease anxiety: activating the left side of your brain.

It is always fascinating to watch the human brain in action. When I have a new client, I always start out with logistics such as paperwork, expectations of counseling, a little about how I operate as a therapist. During this time, my new client may be a little nervous, but their emotions are steady. When we have checked all the legalities, I typically ask, "What brought you to therapy at this point in your life?" This is when the emotions kick in. I may see tears, anger and frustration, a sense of being overwhelmed and jittery.

What happened that caused this visible shift in energy?

The brain happened.

We have two sides of our brain: the left and the right. The left brain manages all the analytic information, the facts, the strategies. I call it the engineering brain. The right brain is where creativity and emotions live. The best-case scenario is to have an equal balance of the left brain and the right brain.

However, it's impossible to use both sides of your brain at their highest level of functioning. Instead, when the left brain is stimulated with intensity, the right brain is forced to become inactive and falls asleep. Likewise, when the right brain is stimulated with intensity, the left brain is forced to become inactive, and it falls asleep.

Let's look at this as it pertains to anxiety. Anxiety is an emotion (right brain). This emotion is fed by thoughts based on fiction and fantasy. These thoughts are our most creative, worst-case scenarios and are often led by the words "what-if."

For example, we probably don't have anxiety today because we ask ourselves, "Oh my gosh, what if I lost my job *yesterday*?" I'm guessing you didn't lose your job yesterday, and if you did, I apologize for this example causing a trigger. But for those of us who did not lose our job yesterday, this potential for anxiety is squished dead in its tracks. Yesterday already happened.

So, our left-brain kicks in and replies, "Yeah, but I didn't lose my job yesterday."

Our right brain might give one more attempt and say, "Yes, but what if you did lose your job yesterday?"

At this point, the game becomes boring, and our right brain gives up because there is no drama to be had.

However, what if the right brain were to say, "OK, but what if you lose your job *tomorrow*?" The right brain is back at the playground and can take that anxiety provoking thought and run with it.

Now, our left brain is going to be completely overwhelmed because tomorrow hasn't happened, and our left brain doesn't know how to manage ideas that haven't happened yet. Good night, left brain!

This gives all kinds of room and energy for the right brain to go bananas with this statement. This what-if thought sparks more fantasy-based ideas. Excitedly, our brain says, "And if you lose your job tomorrow, you're not going to be able to pay your bills. And then your partner will probably leave you. You'll likely lose your car and your home and probably end up on the street in a box, and then what is your family going to think of you? Everyone will be so embarrassed, you'll lose all your friends. And isn't winter coming? What if you end up dying there in the street all alone?"

Oh, my goodness! What do you think is happening inside your body? The release of adrenaline and cortisol flows like a raging river through your limbs. The longer you entertain those thoughts, the higher your anxiety goes, and suddenly you find yourself in a panic attack.

Stop! What is the plan we've been talking about in this chapter?

1. You become aware that you are experiencing the emotion of anxiety.
2. You recognize that you're doing the short, shallow breathing, and you shift your breathing patterns into breathing deeply.
3. You activate your left brain as fast as you possibly can.

Let me introduce you to some practical left brain activities that have proven effective for anxiety relief, both for me and my clients. You might need to repeat and mix these activities until your left brain kicks in. Once that happens, you'll likely experience a calming effect, as it prompts your right brain to dial down its intensity and step away from the mental spotlight.

Self-Reflection #4: Left Brain Activation Tricks

Here is a list of techniques for you to activate the left brain.

- Take the alphabet, A to Z, and come up with any of these variations that correlate with each letter.
    - Animals at the zoo; for instance, A= antelope, B= bear, and so forth. By about the letter "G," you have to start actually thinking, "What is at the zoo that starts with 'G?'" Hello, left brain!
    - You can use people's names.
    - You can use states and their capitals.
    - You can use restaurants you have visited.
    - You can use types of cars.

Just make sure everything follows the order of the letters of the alphabet.

- Take the colors of the rainbow and come up with foods that go with each color.
- Look around the room and count how many people have blond hair, how many have a dress on, how many have a purse or briefcase, how many people are wearing a red shirt, and so on. Anything that requires you to focus on a detail and count is using the left brain.
- A game on your phone can help. I play solitaire, sudoku, and a crossword game called Word Crossy.
- Any math or accounting problems.
- Go over all the addresses of the places you lived or worked. Your birthday, your family members' birthdays.
- Count backward from one hundred by sevens.

You can also google "ways to activate the left-brain" for many more techniques. Find whatever works for you, but remember that this is step three of the six-step process to calm anxiety.

STEP 4- APPLY COGNITIVE DISCIPLINE

This is the meat and potatoes! I am well aware of the fact that you are probably saying, "Tami, but I still have this problem, this nagging issue, this traumatic memory. I still have this thing that results in my feeling anxious, and you haven't even addressed what to do with it!" I know, I hear you, but I have a method.

So many times, I meet with my clients, and they want to dive head-first into their trauma. I have met with rare clients who can do this and not end up in complete panic, but for most of us, it would be dangerous and irresponsible of me to encourage that. It would be like throwing someone who can't swim into the deep end of an ice-cold pool.

So, we must first become aware, breathe with intention, activate the left, logic minded brain, and now, my friend, you have prepared your body to deal with the issue. It's time to tap into the cognitive aspect and understand where these thoughts lost control.

I want to give you a few ways to apply cognitive discipline and gain insight into what is behind the panic space, but don't try these techniques in the same sitting. Pick one and give it a shot. Utilize what you learn and implement it for a week or so. Then feel free to try another technique.

Self-Reflection #5: The 5%-90%-5% Method

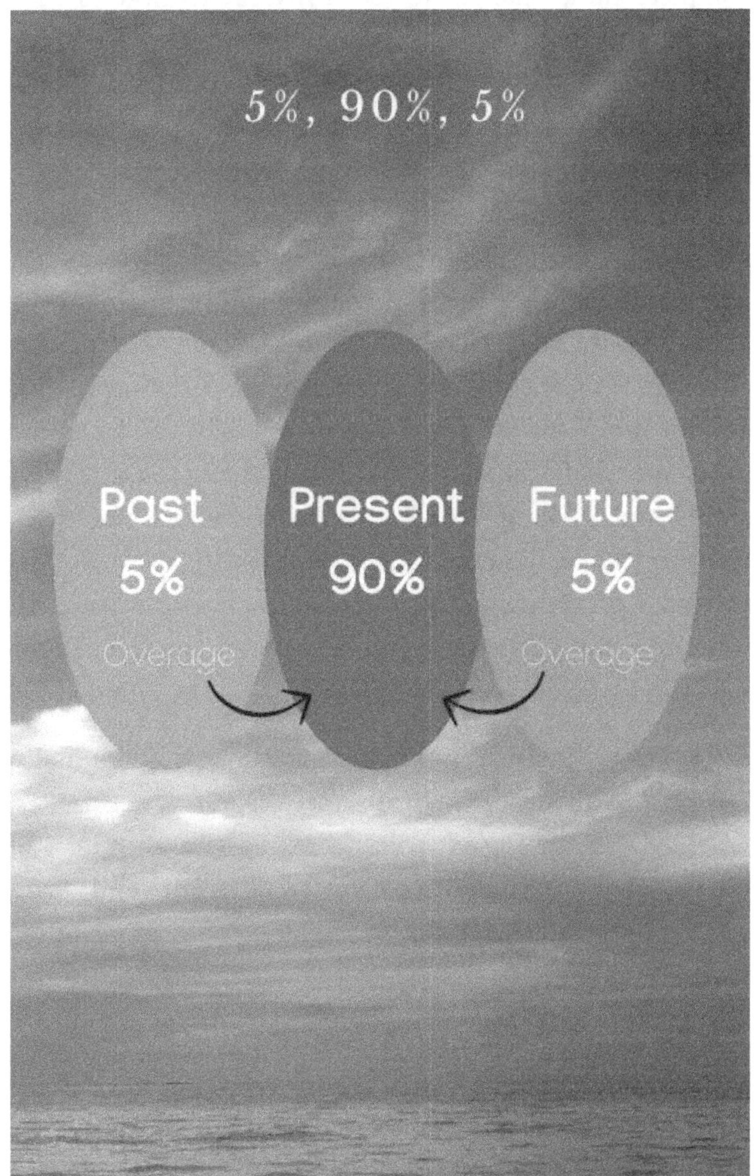

When I developed this next exercise, I realized it was a complete game changer to teach my clients how to gain control and discipline cognitive thoughts. Because I like tangible ideas and the use of analogies to put understanding to my thoughts, I came up with something that uses the body sensations as well as the mind.

I'd like to introduce you to the 5%–90%–5% technique.

Remember in Chapter One, when I said that body has a first reaction, then the mind has a thought, and then the behavior is the result? The 5%–90%–5% begins with paying attention to your body as it pertains to the past, the present, and the future. Follow these instructions and you will most likely feel relief of anxiety while also applying cognitive discipline and working through this anxiety. Now when I refer to a percentage, I am not relying on scientific proven odds; instead, I am giving you a reference. You must ask yourself, what does this particular percentage of energy feel like for me? We are all different, but please use this as a guide.

1. Get a piece of unlined paper, turn it horizontally and divide it into thirds. (see diagram).
2. Label the far-left column as "Past" and write 5%, label the middle column as "Present" and write 90%, and label the far-right column as "Future" and write 5%.

The goal is to become aware of the energy in your body and learn to place 90% of your energy in the present moment. Think of the 5% energy in the past and 5% energy in the future as guard rails. They provide a cushion, so you don't go off the edge. Instead, if you accidentally allow the energy to flow over this 5%, you want these guard rails to bump you back into the center, to the present, where you are most at peace internally. I'll explain.

Let's start with the far-left column, your past. If you spend a healthy 5% of your energy in the past, it allows you to have awareness of what you have been through, mistakes you have made, successes for which you worked hard. When you think about your past and feel a heaviness, an unsettledness, a slipping out of control, your body is speaking to you. Maybe even yelling.

The 5% of energy allows you to assess your past and determine if you want to make that mistake again. You may feel a little guilty or a little shameful, but that's okay. This means you care and that you have a conscience. If you made some major mistakes and didn't have any guilt or shame, that would be weird. However, this is the time where you can recognize it (awareness) and understand that 5% is okay. You can sit with this and feel your feels. In a minute, you are going to take action with this 5% of guilt and shame or any other emotion that pops up.

However, if you allow the mind to travel beyond the 5%, you will likely feel a stronger sense of guilt, shame, and fear. Your thoughts will take you down the blame tunnel. Since you can't go back and change the situation, and you will never forget it, this spiral of negative energy will cause a great deal of anxiety and guilt over something that has already happened and that can never change.

3. Take twenty seconds and on the left column, jot down memories that pop into your mind about situations you just can't let go of from your past. These memories could be something you did to someone else or something someone has done to you. These memories could be mistakes and bad decisions that you regret.

4. Now bring awareness to your body. How do you feel? As you have taken this time and allowed your thoughts to travel back in space, the body may begin to feel unsettled. This is one reason I suggest taking twenty seconds to reminisce and not twenty minutes. Otherwise, you'd automatically go way beyond the 5% and spin off the mountain. Stick with me!

5. Now, you will practice thought stopping. Breathe. Pick one memory to work with, and only one.

6. Shift your thinking into the center, 90% energy, the present. Ask yourself these questions and write your answers in the center. You can even draw an arrow from the left side into the center column to indicate to your brain, "We are making a conscious shift."
   a. What was my learning opportunity that came from this event?
   b. What can I do today, at this moment, to assure myself that I will not repeat that situation, or allow that situation to ever happen again?

   c. Remind yourself that you are in your present moment. You are safe. You are not in the past. Breathe deep and long. Exhale slowly.

   d. Repeat to yourself, "That was then, this is now" over and over again.

Now let's move to the far-right side of the paper, your future. If you use 5% of your energy in the future, this allows you to anticipate what is coming around the corner. It allows you to plan and prepare for what you believe may happen. This gives you a sense of control of what you think may happen in your near future. Do you have a test coming up? You can study. Do you have company coming to stay with you? You can clean. You're planning and setting yourself up for success.

In a perfect world, that sounds lovely. Instead, what our right, drama seeking brain does is tempt you to skid right out of that 5% and, like a monkey, go on a wild adventure through the jungle, swinging from vine to vine with all the creativity and what-if's it can conjure up. The body reacts, and you find yourself in a tailspin into anxietyville. But wait…you now have a plan!

   7. Take thirty seconds and, on the right side of the page, jot down some thoughts that take you into your future mind. What are you worried about? What is coming up for you in your life? What are those thoughts that pop in your head while you are trying to sleep? What thoughts cause your palms

to sweat? Remember, you must stick to the thirty-second rule.

8. The goal here is to recognize the what-if and worst-case scenario thoughts, practice the thought stopping, and shift the thinking back to the middle column. Shift your thinking into the center, 90% energy, the present. Ask yourself these questions and write your answers in the center. Again, draw an arrow from the right side into the center column to indicate to your brain, "We are making a conscious shift."

   a. Identify one what-if or worst-case scenario thought to focus on. Only one.

   b. In the middle column, write down three things you will do if that what-if or worst-case idea ever came to fruition.

   c. Next write down three things you are already doing to make sure that a what-if or worst-case idea never comes to fruition.

   d. Remind yourself that you are in your present moment. You are safe. You are not too far ahead in the future. Breathe deeply and long. Exhale slowly.

And now you are back to utilizing 90% of your energy right here in the moment. You feel more focused. Your brain will tempt you to pick another topic to find some drama around. Go ahead and entertain it, but utilize this sequence, and pretty soon, the right brain will get bored that you aren't playing the "Let's have a crisis" game, and it will give in and let go.

9. If you want to work on the middle column and the ideas you came up with around what you learned from the past and/or what you can plan for going forward, you may be able to develop some short-term, realistic goals. You are taking control over your life and increasing your confidence, therefore, decreasing your anxiety.

Self-Reflection #6: Mapping Journal Technique

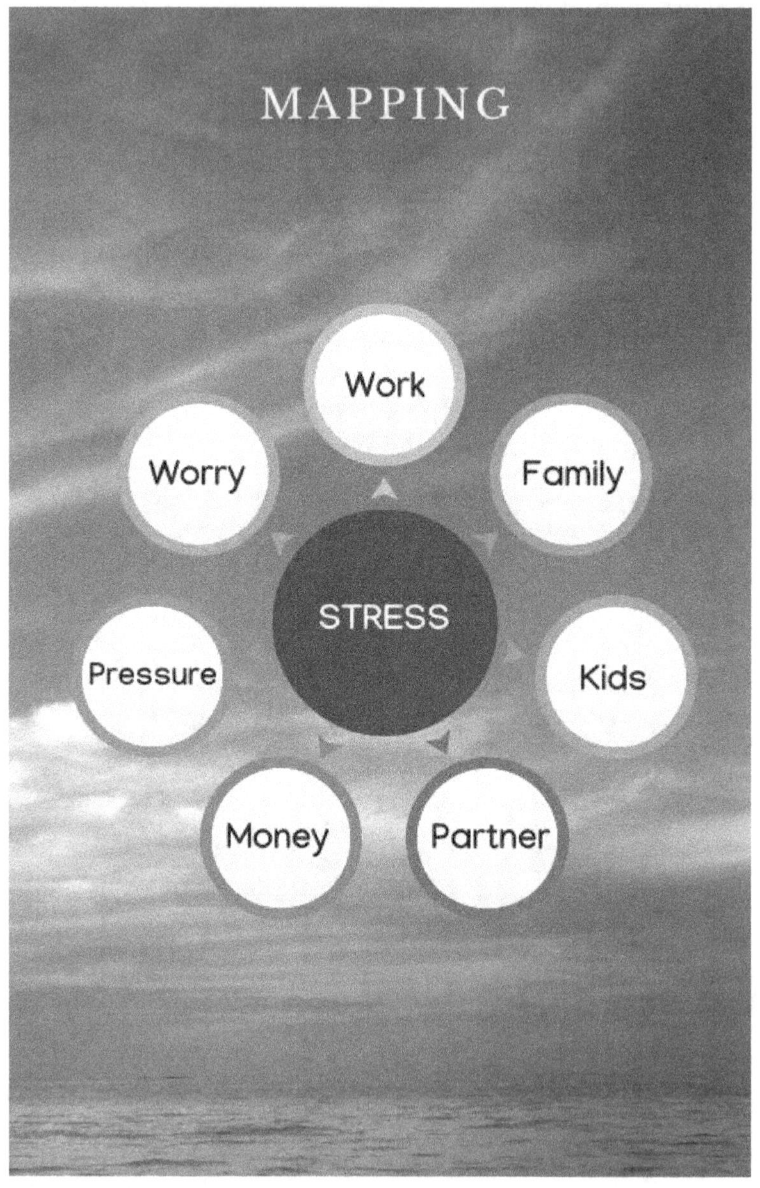

I'm a big advocate for journaling, but I'll admit, I struggle with it myself! Despite my best intentions and owning a gazillion journals, I often find it hard to carve out the time and discipline to journal regularly.

That's why I find this next exercise so impactful. Instead of spending an hour writing detailed entries about my day, I've discovered a quick and powerful alternative. In just five to ten minutes, I can achieve what might take hours of traditional journaling. It's like sprinkling a little magic dust on your routine! You may have heard of mapping. Well, this is mapping with a unique Tami twist.

1. Get a piece of unlined paper and turn it horizontally.
2. Draw a circle in the middle. Write one word in the middle, such as "Stress," "Overwhelm," "Anxiety," or whatever negative feeling you want to vent and seek clarity around. For this example, I am going to use the word "Stress" for the center circle.
3. From your middle circle, draw a line and put another circle at the end of that line. This will be something that causes you stress. For my example, I will call it "Work."
4. Expand on each offshoot by adding more circles and labels. For instance, other topics may include "Family," "Finances," or "Relationship." Draw as many offshoots from the middle circle as you want.
5. Expand on each offshoot by adding more circles and labels. For example, under "Family," I would draw a line and a circle labeling it "Kids," and off

"Kids," I would add "Leaving for College." Another line and circle off "Family" is "Parents," and off "Parents," would be "Aging." Get it?

6. Elaborate in as much detail as possible.

7. Take about three to five minutes to fill out your map.

Cautionary note: you may feel anxious while completing your mapping because you are digging up a lot of issues that you may have neatly tucked away in the corners of your mind. Traditional journaling allows you to buffer the details with filler words. This is just ideas in the raw. So, if you feel anxious at any time, stop, and go on to the next step.

8. Now, step back, take a breath, and get a drink of ice-cold water.

9. Review the initial layer of topics branching from the center circle. Prioritize which topics need to be addressed first by numbering them.

10. Start with number one, the first topic you want to address. Say it's "Family." Go to the most detailed aspect of that topic, so, for this example, it would be "Kids" and "Leaving for College." I would ask myself what it is about college that is making me so stressed? Then I would write down three ways I can manage my stress when it comes to the topic of my kids leaving to college.

11. Repeat this process for each circle, ask yourself why this topic is causing this emotion and what are three things you will do to manage the emotion. Or

you may write down three things you are doing to prevent this topic from happening. For example, under the "Finances" circle, maybe your deepest fear is "Going Bankrupt." What are three things you need to do to manage your money and prevent bankruptcy?

12. Now, you have a list of ideas of what you can do to take control of your life instead of spinning out of control, not knowing where to start, or even pinpointing what is causing so much strife.

Self-Reflection #7: Traditional Journaling

The last idea to apply cognitive discipline to is traditional journaling. I have many clients who hold back from journaling because they buy these gorgeous journals, and they don't want to ruin them. Or their journal has dates, and they feel pressured to write every day so as not to waste pages. Yes, I am guilty of this, too! However, sometimes you have to just get messy and write.

Let it flow. Don't worry about making it look pretty. I call it pack and puke. You've packed all this crap inside your body and your mind. Journaling is a time to puke it all out. Does that sound pretty? No. So, just write.

STEP 5- FOCUS ON THE FACTS

Okay. You're almost there. You have identified the anxious feeling, gotten control over the breath, activated the left brain, and applied cognitive discipline. Now it is time to focus on the fact of what you know to be true.

Because anxiety is filled with fictitious ideas and creativity that could fill up a Stephen King novel, we are bringing it down to what has already taken place. We are applying that left brain and taking the fantasy emotion out of it.

Did you worry you may get laid off from your job? Did it lead to the idea of losing your house and your family and your pride and living in a box? Yes, but are you living in a box right now? No. Did you lose your pride and your family and your house? No. Did you actually lose your job today? No.

On the other hand, if you did lose your job today, your worry isn't, "Oh my gosh, what if I lost my job?" You already did, and that's the fact. Now, you start planning what your next step needs to be. File for unemployment, tidy up your resume, get out there and find your next job.

Whatever your situation is, you must come back to the facts of what you know are true. It is the only way to move forward because you are now dealing with something that actually happened. If you try to deal with a what-if or a worst-case scenario, you don't have anything to work with. It's like trying to capture the wind and tie it in a bow. It's impossible, and that will only frustrate you more.

So now you ask yourself, "What are the facts that I know to be true, and what is my next step and course of action?"

STEP 6- FINDING GRATITUDE

The final step in managing anxiety is to identify gratitude.

Actively practicing gratitude helps you shift your focus away from worries and toward more positive aspects of your life. Instead of dwelling on what's lacking or going wrong, or might go wrong, you recognize the abundance and beauty around you, which boosts your contentment and satisfaction.

This shift can also combat patterns of negative thinking that fuel anxiety. By being intentional about recognizing and seeking out the good in your life, you are training your mind to see the brighter side, fostering a more optimistic outlook.

Moreover, gratitude isn't just good for your mind—it's beneficial for your body, too. Studies show that gratitude practices can lower stress hormones, enhance immune function, and improve sleep quality. By nurturing gratitude, you're not only taking care of your mental health but also supporting your physical well-being in dealing with stress and anxiety.

Incorporating gratitude into your daily routine doesn't have to be complicated. It can be as simple as pausing each day to appreciate the small things like the warmth of sunlight, the laughter of someone you love, the beauty of nature, the slurpy kiss from your dog. Creating a habit of gratitude will help to build resilience for stressful times and help you to find peace.

Self-Reflection #8: Mapping with Gratitude

To delve into your gratitude, you can go back to Self-Reflection #2 and complete a map but use the word "Gratitude" for your middle circle. List all the aspects and sub aspects of things, people, pets, and so on of what you are grateful for.

Complete some of the breathing techniques and take in all the gratitude. Let it sink into every muscle and fiber of your being.

Self-Reflection #9: Extend the Love

Go do something for someone else. Pay it forward. This will help you get out of your own head and thoughts. It's hard to have anxiety when you are doing something kind for someone else. You can also show gratitude in this way.

This completes the six-step process of one of the most powerful ways I have found to combat anxiety. Step by step, you will create a new habit for yourself, which will lead to you feeling more confident, stable and in control of your life. I hope this works for you as well as it has worked for me!

CHAPTER FIVE

THE CHAOS TO CALM STRATEGY IN ACTION

PUTTING THE STRATEGY INTO ACTION—CASE EXAMPLE #1

HERE'S AN EXAMPLE OF how I walked a client through this process so you can see how to apply it to your life with your own anxiety provoking situation.

Sarah is a client who entered therapy to try and understand why she suddenly started experiencing a debilitating level of anxiety during the happiest time in her life. She is content in her career and continues to move up the ladder in her company. She has an amazing circle of friends, and she and her boyfriend of four years recently bought a home and moved in together, something they had talked about and strategically planned. Sarah is stable with her finances and lives a very comfortable life, so these sudden panic attacks were confusing. They made her second guess everything she'd worked so hard for.

The way Sarah's anxiety symptoms manifested was even more of a surprise. She became extremely jealous and distrustful of her boyfriend. When he would chat with a female coworker, Sarah immediately went to a worst-case scenario that he was forming a relationship with this other woman. If her boyfriend said he was going to a friend's house, Sarah would drive by to make sure his car was there. She'd never behaved in a way like this. The more she tried to control her impulsive thoughts, the worse it got.

After we discussed more about Sarah's childhood, she described dynamics parallel to avoidant and anxious attachment style. Her father struggled with drug addiction and was in and out of jail. Her mother was extremely passive and lacked the ability to set boundaries with him. Sarah witnessed her father physically and verbally abuse her mother. She learned quickly to hide in her room to avoid the chaos in the home. Her parents stayed married, but Sarah said she'd always wished her mom would have taken her and left her dad.

Sarah's role was flipped with that of her parents. Instead of her being the child, she assumed a parent role to her mother. Her mom would have panic attacks and emotional breakdowns, and, from a very young age, Sarah had to take care of most duties around the house, including laundry, cooking, and getting herself ready for school.

When a child grows up with avoidant and anxious attachment, they learn to not trust other people or their environment. Sarah often found herself in survival mode as a child and adolescent. She learned to only rely on herself, and she had very surface-level relationships with people, since she mostly kept to herself.

It's common that a person in this scenario would develop a very self-centered, even narcissistic personality, but Sarah had a saving grace—her grandmother. It is said that if a child growing up in a chaotic household has at least one supportive adult figure offering consistent, unconditional love, the child has a chance at developing healthy relationships internally and externally.

Sarah didn't exhibit the typical lack of empathy many have in situations like hers. She also did not exhibit a history of anxiety, which was peculiar, given her lack of control over her environment in her home. However, Sarah's coping mechanism became self-determination. She graduated from high school with honors while working a part-time job. She got herself in college, self-paid, graduated, and landed a job where she had been for fourteen years when she became my client. She learned to never rely on anyone to make her happy or successful. She learned to not trust others or count on them for consistency.

After a series of short-term romantic relationships that Sarah typically ended when they became "too much," she took a sabbatical from dating. And as the story often goes, this is when she met the boyfriend that she's with now.

After a few sessions in therapy, we determined that this is the first time Sarah has ever allowed herself to be vulnerable in a relationship. Because she never learned to trust others or experienced anything about healthy conflict resolution, Sarah's anxiety was the result of fear: fear that her boyfriend would leave her, that he'd find someone else, that he'd realize all her flaws and want nothing to do with her.

When I met Sarah, she was very matter-of-fact when recalling events of her childhood. This was an indication she had compartmentalized so much of the abandonment and rejection she longed for. She spoke from her left brain, with strategy and a fact base. However, as she described her boyfriend's behavior as kind, warm, understanding, and loving toward her, she became emotional. When she described how she had followed him to check his story, yelled at him for talking with a female coworker, and accused him of cheating on her with his female best friend from high school, I watched Sarah unravel. She was appalled at her own behavior toward him.

If we were going to work through her imagined thoughts of her boyfriend cheating, we had to utilize the 5%–90%–5% technique.

Because Sarah's left brain, the logical, fact based side of thinking, was completely shut down, she couldn't regroup and identify how her thoughts were spiraling into fantasy based ideas. Then her body was reacting as if these thoughts were actually occurring, and panic set in.

- Step one: gain awareness of the emotion. In this case, that emotion is anxiety.
- Step two: control the breath. I asked Sarah to gain awareness of her inhale and exhale. We used the technique of inhaling the cool air and exhaling

warm air. When her breath was regulated, we moved on to the next step.

- Step three: activate the left brain. I started asking Sarah questions about her new home. I asked her to describe the view while she sat at her kitchen window. I asked how many trees she had in her backyard. I asked how she set up her office. I asked how long it took her to drive to work. As I asked Sarah more questions about left brain topics, I watched the color come back into her face. I heard the tone in her voice calm and saw the tears disappear from her eyes. Then I pointed out what just happened. She activated her left brain, which automatically calmed the right brain. I actually got a giggle out of her.

- Step four: cognitive processing. It was clear that Sarah was using 45% of her energy in the past, 45% of her energy in the future and 10% of her energy in the present. A very unhealthy balance.

When Sarah looked into her past, she could identify how her upbringing affected her ability to trust others and to be vulnerable. She was able to identify the enormous amount of guilt she felt for treating her boyfriend with such distrust and anger. She felt guilty about not "fixing" her parents and not doing enough for them. She recognized she'd been hiding behind the wall of defensive behavior that she built to keep herself safe, and even felt guilty about building said wall. We worked to understand the fine line of her having control over guilt versus the guilt having control over her, which would lead to anxiety and panic.

Sarah was able to shift the amount of energy she was wasting in the past over things she couldn't change, living with guilt and a sense of never being good enough, to where she was in the present moment. She was able to gain awareness of everything she did to try and help her parents, including how she took control of her life in the best way she could, focusing on her school and career. And she was able to see that her wall of defense was built as a protection, but she was also able to lower it and build a romantic relationship with her boyfriend.

Sarah was also able to recognize that because she lacked the ability to trust that anyone would unconditionally love her, she was always waiting for the other shoe to drop, waiting for her boyfriend to leave her. She was able to keep this fear under a weighted blanket, stuffed in the corner of her closet, until she and her boyfriend moved in together. This is when the relationship became "real" in her mind, and suddenly she had more to lose. She realized that fear of being rejected and abandoned had been tucked away and waiting for the right time to strike. Bam, there it was.

We were able to pull that energy back to the present. Sarah acknowledged that even if her worst-case scenario idea of her boyfriend leaving would be devastating, she knew she had been alone before in her life, and she would adjust. This related to identifying how you would manage if your worst-case scenario idea came true. She wasn't dependent on him. She was also able to identify that she had developed healthy communication with her boyfriend. They talked about areas of conflict and were able to find resolutions while becoming even closer. She realized she had allowed a vulnerability to create a trusting foundation with her boyfriend. This related to identifying what she was doing to prevent her worst-case scenario idea from coming true.

Sarah found herself in a place of trust within herself that she hadn't ever revealed. Slipping out of survival mode and into living mode was a new space for her, and although it caused a disequilibrium in her cognitive through process, she realized she'd become comfortable in something that was unhealthy but a habit.

- Step five: the facts. Sarah listed all the facts in her relationship that she knew to be true. Her boyfriend was patient, and he answered her questions. He wanted to understand where her fears were coming from so he could offer reassurance. They had excellent communication, and a strong degree of trust had already been established. They both respected and appreciated each other.
- Step six: find gratitude. When Sarah thought about her relationship with her boyfriend, it was like watching the fog dissipate from a window on a sunny morning. The warmth of gratitude brought tears to her eyes as she realized that she had never experienced such a healthy, loving connection before. Her anxiety, once a looming presence, now

seemed to vanish into thin air, leaving her feeling lighter and freer than ever before.

PUTTING THE STRATEGY INTO ACTION—CASE EXAMPLE #2

Ryan is a thirty-eight-year-old male client who came to me for help with debilitating anxiety. He is a successful software programmer who works for a large corporation. He loves his job but has been close to getting fired on several occasions for not showing up to work. His employer has no idea about how paralyzing his anxiety can be.

After getting to know Ryan, I deemed his diagnosis as post-traumatic stress with the presence of dissociative symptoms. Let me explain.

Ryan reported being the victim of physical, emotional, and sexual abuse as a child. He was isolated in a small town and did not have any kind of strong support system in place to help him through this traumatic experience. By the time I met him, he had been through several years of trauma focused therapy, but he still experienced dissociating when certain triggers were presented. Ryan's triggers were taking trips home, being near family, working with someone whose behavior reminded him of his abusive father, being under pressure to complete difficult projects in a short time frame, to name a few. He also identified the dissociative symptoms that would occur if he wasn't sleeping.

Dissociative disorders are conditions where there's a kind of "break" or "disconnect" in how our mind works.

This can show up in different ways, like feeling like you're not really yourself (depersonalization), feeling like the world around you isn't real (derealization), forgetting important things (amnesia), feeling unsure about who you are (identity confusion), or feeling like you're a different person at times (identity alteration).

In Ryan's case, his dissociations could last for a month or two at a time. Because he had the option to work from home, he could log onto his workstation, perform the functions he needed to perform, and do quite well at his job. However, he would forget to take his medication or to put food back into the refrigerator. Ryan reported going for weeks without a shower or brushing his teeth. He described his apartment during a dissociative episode as filthy, with moldy food putting off quite a stench. When he finally associated (came back into himself, where his brain would find the appropriate connections again), he would fall into a deep depression at his disbelief of what he'd done to himself, and his home became his reality. He'd become so overwhelmed with anxiety about where to start cleaning up, he'd sometimes go back into a dissociation. He just wanted to live a normal life without these massive disruptions and setbacks.

The fascinating part of how Ryan would cycle through these trauma responses was that he could still work proficiently. Sometimes, he could even drive himself to work. I asked what it was like at work during a dissociation when he likely needed to interact with his peers, but Ryan doesn't remember. He has no recollection of these dissociative periods of time. We'll talk about the reasons as to why Ryan could function at his job during a dissociation when I demonstrate the way Ryan utilized the six-step model.

- Step one: gain awareness of the emotion. In this case, it is anxiety.
- Step two: control the breath. I asked Ryan to gain awareness of the inhale and exhale. We used the technique of inhaling the cool air and exhaling warm air. When his breath was regulated, we moved on to the next step.
- Step three: activate the left brain. Ryan loves to travel and has been all over the world. I asked him to use the letters of the alphabet, starting with A, and tell me all the places he has traveled, correlating the names of the towns, states, or countries with each letter of the alphabet. As Ryan began talking about his travels, he immediately felt the anxiety dissipate and his mind coming into the present moment instead of being triggered by past events and future unknowns.

Ryan's job as a software programmer utilized mostly left brain activity. He was coding and using equations and numbers. He used strategy and analytics to complete tasks at work. This is why he was able to function during a dissociation at work. It was his right brain, the emotional source that was shut down during the dissociation.

- Step four: cognitive processing. Ryan tended to spend about 60% of his energy in the past, 20% in the present and 20% in the future. However, when he dissociated, he was completely checked out of his reality and created an alternate reality which was neither in the past, present, or future. However, his dissociation was caused by his present moment getting triggered by past events. It was even more important for him to train his brain to stay in the present moment, giving him the most control over his dissociation response.

Cognitive processing therapy for Ryan was based on helping him practice recalling individual experiences from his past, and immediately helping him identify his present situation. We would practice this because, as I've indicated before, the brain will always show up to protect you, even though it doesn't know if the idea is a perceived event or an actual event. When Ryan would get triggered, by say a movie, a song, or a smell, for example, his brain would immediately flip into protective mode, indicate a warning sign, and dissociate, basically checking out and taking a hiatus from his reality. Over time, Ryan became skilled at checking in with himself and practicing techniques to assure he was spending 90% of his energy in the present moment. This allowed him to also practice preparation techniques for when he did talk with family members or even take a trip home. He was preparing his brain to remember that the past is the past. A coping statement we used was, "That was then. This is now". This is a useful and simple coping statement for people who have experienced trauma in their lives.

For Ryan, step one, awareness, was key in forcing his brain to associate and stay in his current reality.

Over time, Ryan has been able to process through many of the traumatic events he endured as a child. Instead of ignoring these memories and compartmentalizing them away, he has gained the confidence that he can recall an event while still maintaining control over his emotions and his cognitive structure.

- Step five: facts. Maintaining the awareness and present mindset, Ryan can focus on the facts to be true. For him, the facts are that he lives in a different state from where he grew up. He is in control when, in what capacity and for what duration, he talks with his family. He is surrounded by people he trusts and feels comfortable to be vulnerable around. These facts remind Ryan that his current environment is safe, and he has control over his life.

- Step six: gratitude. Because Ryan has been able to work through his trauma, he has found a sense of gratitude for the freedom he feels by being able to break the heavy chains he once felt in connection with his past. He has also worked extremely hard to find forgiveness for his abusers. He knows that forgiveness doesn't mean that the abuse was okay, but that it allows him to find peace internally. He is no longer a slave to his past. He knows that his identity is not that of what happened to him, but he was a victim of someone else's awful behavior. He has also been able to identify generational abuse and trauma that his perpetrators experienced, which has allowed him to have a sense of compassion. Again, he is not excusing the behavior, but detaching from its destructive clenches.

By seeing how just two case examples can utilize the 5%–90%–5% and six-step model, you can now step back and take note of your own situation. Choose an experience that you struggle finding peace with and write in your journal how you can apply this method.

CHAPTER SIX

CELEBRATE - EMBRACE THE POWER OF ANXIETY

AS COUNTERINTUITIVE AS IT may sound, there is a hidden strength within anxiety, a force that propels us forward, keeps us vigilant, and even protects us from harm. In this chapter, we'll delve into the often-overlooked aspect of anxiety—its positive potential. While anxiety is commonly associated with distress and discomfort, it also serves as a powerful motivator, a guardian of our well-being, and a catalyst for growth.

Imagine anxiety as a trusted ally, standing guard at the gates of our mind, alerting us to potential threats, and urging us to take action. It's the surge of adrenaline that heightens our senses in moments of danger, the voice of caution that whispers warnings in times of uncertainty. Far from being a mere nuisance (or, at times, a complete disability in life), anxiety can be a vital tool in navigating life's challenges and seizing opportunities.

In this chapter, we'll explore the ways in which anxiety can serve as a source of strength and resilience. You'll learn to recognize its positive manifestations, harness its energy, and transform it from a hindrance into a helper. By reframing your perception of anxiety and embracing its inherent power, you can cultivate a newfound sense of empowerment and resilience in the face of adversity. Let's unlock the hidden gifts that anxiety has to offer.

First of all, remember that anxiety is just an emotion, like happiness, joy, fear, jealousy, excitement, sadness, and so on. I don't know about you, but for me, sometimes just hearing the word "anxiety" can cause my heart to skip a beat. All emotions are contagious. If you walk into a room filled with happy, motivated, like-minded people, you probably can't help but get a little excited, too. Likewise, if you walk into a room of anxious people who are freaking out and losing their minds over something, that lands on you, and you probably will end up sharing their panic.

I would like to remind you of this because we attach a reaction to an emotion. We think that having jealousy is an awful thing, but it can be an opportunity for self-reflection and to help us shift something in our lives that isn't working. What about feeling failure? Failure often carries a stigma of disappointment and inadequacy. However, it provides valuable lessons and opportunities for growth. Each failure offers a chance to learn from mistakes, refine strategies, and develop resilience. It can lead to innovation, creativity, and eventual success as we adapt and persevere through setbacks.

We need to learn to treat anxiety equally to these other emotions by giving ourselves permission to feel it. We live in a world where we are so quick to try and fix these "problematic" emotions, to stuff them away, and avoid any painful reactions. While I believe in psychopharmacology, I do not support taking medication without coupling it with psychotherapy, since just throwing medication at a problem won't make it go away. We need to feel what our body is trying to scream at us, when it's begging us to pay attention to it.

People don't usually call me up as a psychotherapist and say, "Hi, Tami, I think I'm getting ready to have a crisis, and I need some preventive help." Instead, I typically get the call saying, "I am in crisis now and need your first available appointment." That's okay, because I've done it, too! Similarly, if you go to a psychiatrist, you will very likely walk out with a prescription because you typically visit a psychiatrist when you think you're at your wits' end. There is no magic pill out there. The purpose of medication is to help the way it was designed to, which then allows you to put the work in and do your part to alleviate the disturbing emotion. This means feeling it, working through it, allowing it to be there, finding peace with it, and moving forward. By looking at the negative and positive aspects of anxiety, you will be able to work the process and find your peace.

BEING AN OBSERVER

From the moment you wake up in the morning, until the moment you fall asleep at night, you are interacting with your environment. The alarm goes off, jolting you out of the depths of a dream, and your first thought may be, "Thank God, that was a horrible dream," or "I hate mornings, I just need at least two more hours of sleep." Either way, there is a reaction, an emotion, and a judgment that are tied to that blaring sound that rattled your innards.

You drive to work and have several judgments about the drivers around you. "A turn indicator would be a great way to let others know your intentions," "Sure, come on over into my lane, you asshole," "Gas pedal on the right, dude!" More judgments, but also more anxiety.

All day long, we react, sometimes negatively, sometimes positively. But each interaction affects our energy. If your day starts off with the heart-stopping alarm, leading to a criticism-filled drive to work, how do you think your energy is when you open your laptop and begin interacting with people? There is a snowball effect of events, judgments, and energy.

If you aren't aware of this emotionally reactive snowball turning into an avalanche, you will likely find yourself exhausted by lunchtime and ready for a drink by five. After scowling and using hand gestures to other drivers on the way home, you plop yourself onto the couch with that long-awaited glass of wine, grab some cereal for dinner, and you're off to bed.

Sound familiar? Time to snap out of it, because I have another option for you.

Observe, do not judge. In moments of quiet observation, we can free ourselves from the grip of anxiety. By stepping back from our emotions and simply watching our thoughts without getting caught up in them, we open ourselves to a sense of calm and understanding. In this peaceful state, we rise above our worries and fears and find a deep sense of clarity and inner strength.

Self-Reflection #1: Bring Awareness to Judgement

1. Make it a point to gain awareness of every single time you make a judgment about a situation in a day. I suggest taking it hour by hour, or fifteen minutes by fifteen minutes. Use tally marks to track every single time you judge.

2. After getting over the shock of how often your mind places a judgment on a situation, a person, even your individual self, evaluate your energy. I suggest doing this evaluation after each hour.

What you will find depends on your mindset: if your energy is light, your judgments are likely positive; if your energy is heavy, your judgments are likely negative.

3. Now practice catching yourself when you make a judgment and turn it into an observation. Based on the examples above, you may instead say to yourself, "That driver did not use a turn indicator," or "That

person merged into my lane without looking," or "That person is going significantly under the speed limit in the left lane." All of these observations could be a sign to stay away from these drivers because they are not practicing safety.

Now, I think I know what you're thinking: you just made a judge-y statement, didn't you? You may even ask, "What is the point?"

When you can watch life happening in front of you and not make a judgment or even a prediction of what could happen in the unforeseeable future, you are maintaining a sense of internal peace. You are an observer, being very picky about what you spend your energy on. When you can choose where your energy flows, you are much more in control of your life. And as you have read several times in this book, when you are in control of yourself and your environment, anxiety is almost non-existent.

SHIFTING TO GET ANXIETY TO WORK FOR YOU

While anxiety is often perceived as a negative emotion, there are ways in which it can be reframed as a positive tool for self-awareness and growth, especially when it reminds us to observe without judgment. Here are some benefits of using anxiety as a reminder to observe.

1. Heightened Awareness: Anxiety can serve as a signal to pay attention to your surroundings and

internal experiences. You will become more attuned to your thoughts, emotions, and bodily sensations. If you are walking down a dark alley at two in the morning (which is another, different conversation), I would hope your anxiety alarms are going off with flashing lights. Your anxiety is helping you have a heightened awareness of your surroundings so you can run or fight if you need to.

2. <u>Mindfulness Practice</u>: Using anxiety as a cue to observe without judgment encourages the practice of mindfulness, which has been shown to reduce stress and improve overall well-being. Being in the moment will help to focus on the facts you know to be true. Mindfulness offers a path to not only awareness, but also acceptance.

3. <u>Emotional Regulation</u>: When you can stay calm, you are in better control. By observing your anxiety without immediately reacting or making judgments, you can develop greater emotional regulation skills, learning to tolerate uncomfortable emotions. Conflict is inevitable in life, but it's important for your reaction to match the situation. This promotes a sense of self-control. You'll manage challenging emotions with greater ease.

4. <u>Cognitive Flexibility</u>: Anxiety can prompt you to adopt a more flexible and adaptive mindset, allowing you to consider alternative perspectives and responses to stressful situations, rather than becoming rigid or fixated on worst-case scenarios.

Think of the reason tall palm trees don't break in gusty winds: they are flexible and not rigid.

5. <u>Increased Self-Compassion</u>: Observing anxiety with compassion and curiosity rather than self-criticism can foster greater self-compassion and self-kindness. This will help you to be gentler and more understanding with yourself during times of stress. Self-compassion leads to stronger confidence.

6. <u>Enhanced Problem-Solving</u>: Anxiety can motivate you to seek out solutions and coping strategies for managing your symptoms. This will lead to improved problem-solving skills and a greater sense of mastery and control over your anxiety. Did you ever procrastinate on a project with a deadline? I'll bet in the early hours of the day it was due, your anxiety shifted into production.

7. <u>Heightened Introspection</u>: Anxiety can prompt you to engage in introspection and self-reflection. This will lead to greater insight into the underlying causes and triggers of your anxiety and facilitate personal growth and self-discovery.

8. <u>Promotion of Growth Mindset</u>: Viewing anxiety as a reminder to observe without judgment fosters a growth mindset, encouraging you to see challenges as opportunities for learning and development rather than insurmountable obstacles.

9. <u>Sense of Urgency</u>: Feeling anxious about a situation can create a sense of urgency to address the situation rather than brushing it off and ignoring

it. What if you felt a migraine headache coming on right when you went to bed at night? You could feel anxiety because migraines can put you out of commission, or you could use that anxiety to get up out of bed and take preventive medication. The urgency causes you to take action while something is manageable rather than procrastinate and wait until the situation becomes a full-on crisis.

To sum up, when we see anxiety as a cue to observe without jumping to conclusions, it can be a catalyst for personal growth. So next time anxiety creeps in, I encourage you to take a moment to observe, without judgment, and see where it leads you on your path. When you start to feel anxiety, go over this list and ask yourself if anxiety is presenting itself for a reason and how you can use it to your benefit.

THE TORNADO IN THE HOTEL HALLWAY

I believe that every seven or eight years we go through a midlife crisis—except it's not always in midlife. When it happens, you'll know it. Your personality stays the same, but you have less tolerance for some aspects of life and more tolerance for others. Your perspective and priorities shift. This change can elicit an anxiety response. I created a visual to help my clients wrap their head around this life-altering experience.

Image that you are in a hotel room. You've been in this space for quite some time and are very comfortable.

You know where everything is: the bed, the drawers, the desk. You have created a routine that feels very comfortable. It has served you well for a few years (seven or eight, if you are like me in my imaginary hotel room). But one day you wake up and you start to feel antsy. Your comfort has turned into restlessness. You're curious about what lies beyond that hotel room door.

So, you decide to peek out.

Shocked and caught off guard, you see a tornado, a whirlwind storm in the hallway. Nothing is predictable. This is your midlife crisis, your seven- or eight-year shift. You aren't sure if you should step out into the hallway or stay in your warm and cozy room. But now that the door is open, you've crossed a point of no return, and you must keep going. The old life isn't even available for you. You have seen too much and already dipped your toe into the next era of life. Of course, you feel anxiety, but this type is called anticipatory anxiety. You are sort of excited to see what waits for you on this next leg of your life journey. This anxiety is motivating, and it alerts you to keep your eyes wide open for opportunities that may not jump right out at you.

As you make your way through the chaotic hallway, you see another door just on the other side. It is open and seems inviting. Half of your body is in the unpredictable hallway, and the other half makes its way into the new room. Nothing is familiar. No routine has been established, but you're very happy to be leaving that crazy hallway. As you struggle to make your way into the new room, you exhale and begin to sort out this next stage of your life.

Congratulations. May you find comfort here for the next seven to eight years.

I like this analogy, and I hope it offers you permission to feel anxiety, to feel the uncertainty of life, and know that it is completely normal. Of course you are unsettled because change is difficult. This is where it wouldn't serve you to find a quick fix to this emotion. Any quick fix will only result in anxiety because now is a time to reflect on what you want this new path to look like. What has served you well in the past to continue, and what has not served you well that you wish to change? What are your new passions and interests?

When I go through these changes in my life, it makes people around me a little bananas, but I can't help it. Neither can you. The key to keeping some type of equilibrium is to try as best to communicate with others what is happening in your psyche. Hopefully your people will be as patient and understanding as mine.

While you're in this space, I encourage you to have self-compassion while you allow yourself to sort out the confusion and check in with yourself about what you need to get settled in. You may feel rushed. That is normal because the discomfort of the unknown makes that inner critic come out in full force. Thoughts you may have look like, "Get your shit together. What is wrong with you?" or, "Here you go again. You're a mess. How many times are you going to disassemble what you already created?" It's okay.

Just acknowledge these thoughts and let them dissolve, like ripples disappearing on a calm lake.

I'd also encourage you to practice gratitude. You can identify what was in the old hotel room that gave you purpose and strengthened your identity. All the experiences you endured in seven or eight years can be significant. Relationships started and maybe ended. Having children and watching all the significant stages they passed through. Jobs and/or friends that came and went. Be grateful for these experiences. How fortunate you were to have loved and lived. Maybe this brings up sadness because there was likely a sense of loss during this era. Feel it. This will help you as you make this transition into the new hotel room.

Self-Reflection #2: Create Your Hallway

1. Draw this visual depicting your transformation. What does your old hotel room look like? What served you well, and what would you like to change as you move forward? What are you grateful for?
2. What does your hallway look like? What aspects create the most anxiety for you, and how are you managing this emotion? Where do these aspects come from, and what do they trigger in you?
3. What does your new room look like? What are your passions that you want to explore? What changes do you want to make based on your previous hotel room? How will you achieve these transformations?

APPLYING THE BULLSEYE – YOU ARE THE CENTER

Another benefit that anxiety has is its ability to help you set boundaries with other people. It can act as a signal that something may be wrong or that your well-being may be at risk.

Meet Meg, a vibrant woman juggling the beautiful chaos of motherhood, marriage, and entrepreneurship. With two energetic kids in elementary school and a part-time business on the rise, Meg's plate is fuller than ever. But behind her cheerful facade lies a struggle that weighs heavily on her shoulders: anxiety.

Meg's family, while well-meaning, often overstep their bounds, dropping by unannounced and monopolizing her weekends with endless family gatherings. When she was growing up, Meg learned that keeping everyone happy was the key to harmony, but as she tries to balance her own needs with those of her loved ones, the pressure becomes suffocating.

With every passing day, Meg finds herself caught in a whirlwind of self-doubt and second-guessing. The confident woman she once was has been overshadowed by a constant fear of disappointing others and a relentless need to please everyone around her.

As she navigates the challenges of motherhood and entrepreneurship, Meg's anxiety reaches new heights, leaving her feeling overwhelmed and exhausted. Despite her best efforts, she struggles to assert her boundaries and carve out time for herself amidst the chaos.

But beneath it all, Meg is determined to reclaim her sense of confidence and find balance in her life. That is why she called me to begin counseling. We began talking about this sense of anxiety she experienced. She reported having more frequent panic attacks, especially when she anticipated her husband beginning to travel again for work. Initially, she was looking for a quick fix to make the anxiety go away. But instead, we are going to take a different approach. Meg's anxiety is showing up as a warning sign that, if she doesn't set limits and place healthy boundaries in her life, her body will continue to scream at her until something gives, and hopefully it isn't her mental and physical well-being.

Let's delve deeper into Meg's journey, where her anxiety becomes a catalyst for change and growth. It's as if her anxiety is sounding an urgent alarm, demanding that she take action now. Through our discussions, Meg begins to recognize that her anxiety isn't just a burden—it's a messenger, urging her to set boundaries with the people in her life, even those she loves dearly.

Together, we explore the idea that Meg's anxiety can be a valuable teacher, guiding her toward an initially daunting concept at first, but one that I encourage Meg to lean into to allow her anxiety to show her the way forward. After all, discomfort often accompanies growth, and Meg is ready to embrace the challenge.

As we navigate this journey together, I remind Meg of the power she holds within herself. Her anxiety isn't a sign of weakness—it's a sign of her strength and resilience. It's a reminder that she has the power to protect herself, to prioritize her own needs, even in the face of discomfort.

With each session, Meg learns to harness the power of her anxiety, using it as a motivator for self-preservation. She begins to recognize when certain people in her life lack boundaries and could potentially take advantage of her vulnerability. Armed with this awareness, Meg takes the necessary steps to protect herself, setting firm boundaries and advocating for her own well-being.

Through it all, Meg discovers a newfound sense of empowerment—a realization that she is capable of navigating life's challenges with courage and grace. Her anxiety, once seen as a hindrance, becomes a source of strength, a guiding light. And as Meg continues to embrace her anxiety as a teacher and a friend, she takes confident strides toward a brighter, more empowered future.

Self-Reflection #3: You are the Bullseye

We will now create a bullseye diagram, so grab your blank piece of paper and turn it horizontally.

1. Draw a dot in the very center of the paper. Continue to draw rings around that dot, creating the image of a bullseye.
2. Imagine yourself at the center of the bullseye. You are the command point. You get to determine

everything that happens around you. Each ring around you, from the closest to the farthest are the boundaries you are setting with other people.

3. I like to use a pencil for the next step because what you will create isn't permanent. There is fluidity and room for adjustment.

4. Now when you think of the people in your life who are in your very inner circle, who are they? These are people who you can completely be yourself around. Trust and respect are mutual. Write their names in the inner circle. Reminder: this is not the center. This is your space, and you don't share your individual space. That is yours. The next space out is the first space you share.

5. Go to the second line. Whose names do you place there? It may be people who you are pretty close to but may not share all the details of your life. Write names of people you would like to place in this space.

6. The next line represents people in your life who you share time with but not who you share very personal information with. This may include a neighbor or a teacher at your child's school or a colleague at work. Write the names of the people you want to place here.

7. The following lines are people with whom you rarely share information—either because you don't know them very well, or you have trusted them in the past and they repeatedly violated your trust.

These are the people who lack boundaries and take advantage of your time, energy, and space. Write the names of people you need to place in here.

8. Continue writing names for the rest of the rings you have drawn. Place people where you need to according to what you are needing in your life at this moment.

9. There may be people you just need to flick off the page. You can write their names on the back of the piece of paper. It's important to write their names somewhere because you are setting a hard boundary with them, indicating they are not invited into your space at any time. These are people you have tried to set boundaries with, but they have no intention of your well-being, so out of self-preservation, you no longer allow them in your life. Write those names down on the flipside of your paper.

10. Take a deep breath, step back, and observe your bullseye. How does it feel? Does it feel empowering? It may even feel a little scary because it means you are going to need to practice setting boundaries. You might also feel a little lonely as you realize the company you keep may not have your best interests in mind. All of these feelings are normal and very powerful in their messages.

The reason I encouraged you to write these names in pencil is because based on the day, what you have going on in your life, and your mood, this arrangement may change. It's okay to place your spouse, even your kids on the next line out. Maybe you are requiring more you time. That's fine. Give yourself permission. Sometimes, you set a boundary with a person, and it offers a chance for them to make changes to nurture the relationship. In Meg's case, she set limits with her family telling them she needed a month off from seeing any of them. It sparked a conversation, and they were able to hear her for the first time. She initially moved them to ring number four, but eventually brought them back to ring number two.

The bullseye method helped Meg use her anxiety to make changes in her life. It motivated her to communicate her needs and expectations to the people in her life. Internally, it gave her permission to say no, ask for space, express her opinion, and practice self-care. Her symptoms of anxiety still pop up now and then because she still has a lot on her plate, but she uses this as an opportunity instead of letting the anxiety take her down.

Finally, it's crucial to understand that anxiety isn't just a nuisance: it's a valuable ally in life. While it's easy to perceive anxiety as a burden, it often serves as a powerful catalyst for growth and self-discovery.

Throughout this chapter, we've explored the myriad ways that anxiety can actually be a force for positive change. It prompts us to set boundaries, prioritize self-care, and advocate for ourselves in ways we might not have otherwise. By embracing our anxiety and allowing it to guide us, we tap into a wellspring of resilience and empowerment that propels us forward.

Moreover, anxiety is a reminder of our shared humanity. It's a natural response to the ups and downs of life, a signal that you're alive and engaged with the world around you. Rather than resisting or fearing your anxiety, you can learn to accept it with kindness and curiosity, recognizing it as an integral part of your emotional landscape.

Again, I encourage you to reframe your relationship with anxiety. Pause and listen to its whispers of wisdom. Harness its energy for positive change. By doing so, you will embark on a journey of self-discovery and growth—one that will lead you toward greater authenticity, resilience, and fulfillment.

CHAPTER SEVEN

HEALING PATHWAYS - EXPLORING TREATMENT OPTIONS

UP TO THIS POINT, we've looked at several ways to apply a cognitive behavioral approach to managing anxiety symptoms. But let's shift gears in our exploration of anxiety: treatment options. Here are some varied approaches to treating anxiety, some more traditional and some cutting edge. All have the same goal, and that is to decrease anxiety symptoms so you can find your internal peace and live your life in balance.

From non-medication and holistic approaches to pharmacology or the use of modern technology of apps and online resources, we will go over several methods for you to choose to seek treatment. The goal is to access any treatment approach as soon as possible before anxiety gains an even greater control over your life. The more you avoid dealing with this emotion, the longer it will haunt you and steal your independence.

NON-MEDICATION TECHNIQUES TO REDUCE ANXIETY SYMPTOMS

Using a non-medication technique is usually my first suggestion when I am working with someone struggling with anxiety. As you can see, there are several ways to find relief that don't include taking a pill. The following examples offer longer term methods of anxiety management. These are habits that you will build over time because consistency is the key for success.

1. Meditation: This ancient practice cultivates mindfulness and relaxation, helping to calm the mind and reduce stress. By focusing on the present moment, meditation can help alleviate anxious thoughts and promote a sense of inner peace. You can find meditation practices in several places—podcasts, YouTube, websites, studios, Buddhist temples. Several meditation methods are free, and others come at a price.

2. Counseling: Therapy offers a safe space to explore the root causes of anxiety and develop coping strategies. Through talk therapy, you can gain insights into your thoughts and behaviors, learn healthier ways of coping, and receive support from a trained professional. You can find counseling services through your Employee Assistance Program,

insurance or through a private party. Some religious facilities offer counseling. I recommend going through a licensed counselor, but also doing your research! Just because you go to therapy one time with one counselor doesn't mean you have to stick with them. Make sure you find someone who is a good fit and someone who you connect with. These are your sessions, and you want to get the most out of them with someone you trust.

3. <u>Journaling</u>: Writing down your thoughts and feelings can be incredibly therapeutic. Journaling allows you to process emotions, identify triggers, and gain clarity on underlying issues contributing to anxiety. It's a powerful tool to sort out all of the thoughts and ideas that bounce around in your mind. I have given you a few journaling ideas in previous chapters. There are bullet journals, blank page journals, or journal prompts, to name a few types. Find one that best suits you. Whatever kind you settle on, just write! I have bought journals that were so pretty I didn't want to mess them up, so they ended up collecting dust and got messed up that way instead. It's okay to get messy in your journal. That is what they are for: a place to dump the messy stuff in your mind.

4. <u>Educating Yourself</u>: Knowledge is power when it comes to anxiety. Educating yourself about anxiety disorders, symptoms, and treatment options can help demystify the basis of anxiety. Education

offers you a sense of empowerment and will help you make informed decisions about your mental health. The more information you have, the better you can plot out your plan of attack to deal with the symptoms of anxiety.

5. <u>Listening to Podcasts</u>: Podcasts on anxiety and mental health can be inspiring, validating, and offer practical tips. They provide a sense of connection as well as giving you many ways to view anxiety and how it shows up in life. Podcasts can be a reminder that you're not alone in your struggles. Desiree Grimaldi and I co-host a podcast called " Unguarded Minds". Feel free to check it out.

6. <u>Yoga</u>: Combining physical postures, breathing exercises, and meditation, yoga promotes relaxation and reduces stress. Yoga teaches you the connection between mind and body, and this awareness helps you detect unwanted feelings quickly. The sooner you can recognize anxious feelings, the sooner you can apply a remedy and the sooner you will feel relief. After practicing yoga for several years, I became so passionate about the process I completed my certification to teach. I enjoy weaving concepts of yoga into my psychotherapy practice. When it fits with a client, I will create a yoga sequence for them to take home and practice. The opening of energy channels that yoga provides, coupled with psychotherapy, is an amazing practice and offers endless opportunities for growth.

7. <u>Exercise</u>: Physical activity releases endorphins, neurotransmitters that boost mood and reduce stress. Whether it's going for a run, hitting the gym, or taking a dance class, regular exercise is a powerful antidote to anxiety. I always say, exercise and moving your body can be one of the best medicines ever. Oh, and although they aren't medicine, I'd also say that dog kisses can work miracles as well!

8. <u>Nutrition</u>: A balanced diet including fruits, vegetables, lean proteins, and whole grains nourishes your body and supports mental health. Certain nutrients, like omega-3 fatty acids and magnesium, have been linked to reduced anxiety symptoms. Finding foods that feed your soul and your belly are crucial to maintaining emotional stability. If you do take medication, you need to have a balanced diet to metabolize the medication effectively.

9. <u>Drinking Water</u>: Have you ever looked up the ways water can help the human body? It is utterly fascinating. I recommend conducting an online search for all of water's natural benefits. Staying hydrated is essential for optimal brain function and mood regulation. Dehydration can intensify anxiety symptoms, so be sure to drink plenty of water throughout the day. If you do drink alcoholic beverages, it is even more important to hydrate and use electrolytes. Alcohol is not recommended to deal with mental health issues because it is a depressant

and will intensify anxiety and depression. But if you do drink alcohol, make sure you hydrate.

10. <u>Getting Good Sleep</u>: Sleep is a basic need. Quality sleep is crucial for mental health and emotional well-being. Establishing a bedtime routine, creating a restful sleep environment, and practicing relaxation techniques can improve sleep quality and reduce anxiety. There are several sleep apps to help you fall asleep, stay asleep, and even track your sleep. Here are some techniques I recommend to help you fall asleep.

   A. Any of the left brain ideas we talked about in Chapter Four. The A to Z method, sudoku, counting backwards from one hundred by sevens, to name a few.

   B. Lie down and close your eyes. Inhale and squeeze your feet muscles. Exhale, release the clenched feet. Next, inhale and squeeze your calf muscles. Exhale, release. Inhale, squeeze your quads and hamstrings, exhale release. Use this technique for every part of your body as you work up to the crown of your head. Then take one last deep inhale, squeeze every muscle in your body, exhale, and release. Nighty night!

   C. If you toss and turn and can't fall asleep, don't toss and turn for hours watching the clock. Instead, toss for fifteen minutes. Then get up, go into another room with soft lighting. Get a book and read or journal for fifteen minutes.

Then, go back to bed. If you still toss and turn, only allow yourself to do this for fifteen minutes, go back out to the other room. Continue doing this until you fall asleep. You are training your brain that bed is for sleeping, not tossing and turning. Besides, your mind won't ever calm down when you are watching the clock, if it's anticipating the alarm going off.

D. Write down what is occupying your mind. Once you write it down, your mind feels acknowledged and recognized. It is much easier to calm the brain when you can write down the thoughts. Otherwise, your brain tries to hold on to each and every idea so you don't forget them.

11. <u>Taking Vitamins</u>: Certain vitamins and minerals, such as vitamin D, B vitamins, and magnesium, can play a role in mood regulation and stress management. Taking supplementing to get these nutrients may help alleviate anxiety symptoms. Always check with your doctor to make sure you are supplementing correctly if you take other medications.

12. <u>Homeopathic Approach</u>: Homeopathy uses natural remedies to encourage the body to activate self-healing mechanisms. Remedies like Ignatia and Gelsemium are commonly used for anxiety, providing gentle support for emotional balance. Check out your local Natural Grocers or a store with trained staff to help you find the right homeopathic

approach. Again, check with your doctors to make sure you can use these remedies.

13. <u>Herbal Remedies</u>: Herbs like chamomile, lavender, and passionflower have calming properties that can help reduce anxiety. Herbal teas, tinctures, and supplements offer a natural alternative to pharmaceutical interventions. Again, check with your doctor: not all herbal remedies are safe to take with prescribed medications.

14. <u>Massage</u>: I don't know about you, but I love a full body massage! Massage therapy promotes relaxation, reduces muscle tension, and lowers cortisol (the stress hormone) levels. Working out the kinks that cause tension can calm the mind, resulting in relief from physical and emotional tension. Drink lots of water after a massage.

15. <u>Acupuncture</u>: This ancient Chinese therapy involves inserting thin needles into specific points on the body with the goal of rebalancing energy flow. When the body is triggered by the needles, it releases endorphins and regulates neurotransmitters, which reduces anxiety. Always do your research and seek out licensed acupuncturists.

16. <u>Acupressure</u>: Similar to acupuncture, acupressure targets specific pressure points on the body to alleviate tension and promote relaxation. There is a simplicity about acupressure because you can find pressure points on your own body and use this technique anytime. However, you may also

seek out a trained professional to provide acupuncture sessions.

17. <u>EMDR (eye movement desensitization and reprocessing)</u>: EMDR is a psychotherapy approach that helps process traumatic memories and reduce anxiety symptoms. I have used this technique myself, and it was amazing how much it helped me. EMDR helps to reprocess traumatic experiences and find relief of anxiety. Do your research and make sure you find a trained professional who has been practicing EMDR for a few years. I wouldn't recommend doing EMDR with someone who isn't experienced because of the layers of memories it may uncover.

18. <u>Tapping Techniques</u>: Also known as Emotional Freedom Techniques (EFT), tapping involves gently tapping on specific acupressure points while you focus on a specific memory or idea. Tapping works with specific areas on the body: hands, forehead, cheeks, sides of the arms and legs. The specific technique in conjunction with verbal processing can help you let go of negative energy and help create balance in your mind and body.

19. <u>Self-Care Retreats</u>: Self-care retreats offer a rejuvenating getaway from the daily grind. They often provide structured activities, including rest and relaxation. Retreats can offer a time to focus on your individual situation, reflect, and witness personal growth. You can find a combination of

mindfulness practices and therapeutic workshops taking a holistic approach to promote well-being.

20. <u>Breathwork</u>: Breathwork exercises, such as deep breathing or diaphragmatic breathing, can help calm the nervous system and reduce anxiety symptoms. Use the techniques we explored in previous chapters to promote relaxation and decrease anxiety.

21. <u>Aromatherapy</u>: This is one of my favorites just because there are so many amazing smells that induce an instant calm for me. Many scents, such as lavender, chamomile, ylang-ylang, patchouli, and bergamot, to name a few, have been shown to have calming effects on the mind and body. Aromatherapy involves using essential oils to create a soothing atmosphere and promote relaxation.

22. <u>Grounding Techniques</u>: I use many yoga grounding postures in my private practice with clients to help gain focus and a sense of being in the moment. Grounding postures help you feel anchored to the earth and provide a safe, secure feeling, which also helps alleviate anxious thoughts. Not only can you use a yoga practice to achieve feeling grounded, but you can also use meditation, focusing on all five senses and breathwork.

23. <u>Art Therapy</u>: Art therapy helps you tap into the creative brain while processing through anxiety. You've likely heard of painting, drawing, sculpting as a means of art therapy, but I would also encourage knitting, crocheting, and these types of creative

outlets. Have you heard of Zentangle or Neurographica? My mom introduced these forms of art therapy to me. She has created the most amazing works of art and reports this being her number one calming technique. I believe it! As defined by Pavel Piskarev, founder of Neurographica, Psychology of Creativity Institute, "Neurographica is built on scientific principles using the knowledge of visual thinking in combination with the laws and patterns identified by various schools of psychology. Namely: neuropsychology, analytical psychology, Gestalt psychology, Psychosynthesis, social psychology and modern management theory."[3]. Fascinating anxiety management techniques!

24. <u>Music Therapy</u>: The magic of music! Music has the power to evoke emotions, soothe the mind, and reduce stress. Music has the ability to shift your mood on a dime. Have you ever been listening to one song and felt sad and down, only to feel happy and start dancing with the very next tune? Now that is power! I have several playlists on my phone labeled "Calm," "Happy," "Dance," and "Workout." I suggest putting similar playlists on your phone so they are readily available when needed.

25. <u>Nature Therapy</u>: Driving from the city to your nearest natural place will offer an instant ability to

---

[3] "About us," Neurographica Psychology of Creativity Institute, accessed October 13, 2024, https://www.neurographica.us/about

exhale and find calm. Spending time in nature has been shown to reduce anxiety and stress levels. You likely don't need to go far. Take a walk in the park, find a hiking trail, or just sit by a lake or river. Allow yourself to soak in the many benefits of nature to soothe your soul.

26. <u>Animal-Assisted Therapy</u>: Every experienced puppy therapy? Dogs, cats, horses, goats, llamas, you name it. Animals have a special way of bringing joy and calming our nervous system. Animals provide relaxation through touch, play, or just being in their presence. Specific locations provide specialized animal therapy. Google some businesses in your area and check them out. The connection with an animal is priceless.

As you can see, there are so many non-medication techniques that are available from your living room all the way across the world. I encourage you to chose one to start with that connects with your unique lifestyle and personality. Add as many of these to your anxiety-relieving toolkit to help reclaim your calm and manage anxiety symptoms.

TECHNOLOGY OPTIONS TO HELP MANAGE ANXIETY SYMPTOMS

New apps are popping up every day. I am always on the hunt for the new anxiety-relieving tech options that are being developed. As I write this book, here are some popular options and the features they offer.

1. <u>Calm</u>: Calm is a meditation and mindfulness app that offers guided meditation sessions, breathing exercises, sleep stories, and soothing music to promote relaxation and reduce stress. It also features programs focused on topics like stress reduction, gratitude, and self-compassion.

2. <u>Headspace</u>: Headspace provides guided meditation and mindfulness exercises designed to help users cultivate a sense of calm and focus. It offers themed meditation packages on topics such as stress, sleep, anxiety, and relationships, as well as courses to help develop mindfulness skills.

3. <u>Insight Timer</u>: Insight Timer is a meditation app that offers a diverse library of guided meditations, music tracks, and talks from mindfulness teachers and meditation practitioners around the world. It also includes features such as customizable meditation timers, progress tracking, and community forums.

4. <u>Breathe</u>: Breathe is a relaxation app that offers guided breathing exercises and visualizations to help reduce anxiety and promote relaxation. It provides a variety of breathing patterns and allows users to customize their breathing sessions based on their preferences and needs.

5. <u>Moodfit</u>: Moodfit is a mood-tracking and mental health app that allows users to monitor their emotional well-being and track symptoms of anxiety, depression, and other mood disorders. It also offers

tools and resources to help users develop coping strategies and improve their mental health.

6. <u>Happify</u>: Happify is a happiness and resilience app that offers activities and games based on positive psychology principles to help users reduce stress, build resilience, and cultivate a positive mindset. It features exercises focused on gratitude, mindfulness, and emotional regulation.

7. <u>Talkspace</u>: Talkspace is a therapy app that connects users with licensed therapists for online counseling and support. It offers messaging therapy, video sessions, and live chat with therapists, making mental health care more accessible and convenient.

8. <u>Woebot</u>: Woebot is a chatbot-based therapy app that uses cognitive-behavioral techniques to help users manage anxiety, depression, and other mental health challenges. It provides personalized guidance, support, and tools for self-reflection and emotional regulation.

9. <u>Day One</u>: Day One is a versatile journaling app available for iOS, macOS, and Android devices. It allows you to create text entries, add photos and videos, and customize your journal with tags, themes, and reminders. Day One also features end to end encryption for privacy and security.

10. <u>Journey</u>: Journey is a cross-platform journaling app that syncs seamlessly across devices, including iOS, Android, Mac, and Windows. It offers a clean and intuitive interface for writing daily entries,

organizing thoughts, and reflecting on emotions. Journey also supports multimedia entries, including photos, videos, and audio recordings.

11. Penzu: Penzu is a private online journaling platform that prioritizes security and privacy. It allows users to create password-protected journals and encrypt their entries for added security. Penzu offers customizable journal templates, unlimited storage, and the ability to sync across devices.

12. Reflectly: Reflectly is a journaling app that uses artificial intelligence to provide personalized prompts and insights based on users' entries. It offers a simple and intuitive interface for writing daily reflections, setting goals, and tracking mood patterns. Reflectly also includes features like mood tracking, gratitude prompts, and mindfulness exercises.

13. Daylio: Daylio is a mood- and activity-tracking app that incorporates journaling features to help users understand patterns and triggers related to their emotions. It allows users to log daily activities, track mood fluctuations, and add notes to reflect on their experiences. Daylio also offers customizable reminders and statistics to visualize trends over time.

14. Diaro: Diaro is a multi-platform journaling app that offers a range of features for organizing and documenting daily life. It allows users to write text entries, add photos and locations, and categorize entries with tags and colors. Diaro also supports

cloud syncing and backup, ensuring that journal entries are accessible across devices.

15. <u>My Wonderful Days</u>: My Wonderful Days is a simple and user-friendly journaling app that focuses on capturing moments of gratitude and positivity. It encourages users to write daily entries about the things that bring them joy, along with photos and emoticons to express emotions. My Wonderful Days also includes mood-tracking and calendar integration features.

As you can see, technology has a little something for everyone. When you combine these options listed above with the non-medication techniques, you might just surprise yourself by how quickly you can take control over the anxiety symptoms without the need for prescription meds. Better yet, you are developing coping strategies instead of masking the issue with medication.

MEDICATION TECHNIQUES FOR REDUCING ANXIETY SYMPTOMS

Here are a few disclaimers to review. I cannot recommend or prescribe any medications to you. Please consult your doctor for a thorough examination first. I also strongly encourage the combination of psychotherapy and medication therapy and not just medication alone. Although you will feel relief from anxiety symptoms with the correct medication, I believe in working through the root causes of the anxiety you feel. Otherwise, you may continue to have bouts of anxiety and not understand why the recurring, uncomfortable feelings just won't go away. Additionally, medication should be prescribed and monitored by a qualified healthcare professional to ensure safe and effective treatment. If at any time you are feeling suicidal while taking any of the medications prescribed, call a doctor and seek help immediately. If you take a medication route, remember that meds are supposed to make you feel better, not worse, and you must communicate effectively with your doctor about all of the side effects and results of the meds you take.

It may sound as if I am deterring you from seeking medication treatment for anxiety, but I am not. Many clients I work with take medication, and it has done wonders for their ability to relieve anxiety, depression, and mood disorders. Some found benefits from a shorter-term use, something like six months to a year, after which they decrease their dosage, and use the skills they have learned to manage symptoms. Some clients will be on meds for the long-term because they have a genetic factor that requires help. There is absolutely a time and place for meds.

However, I see people jumping to meds as a quick fix and I watch how they become reliant on meds instead of using their own ability to understand where anxiety resonates and develop healthy coping strategies. That is why I urge you to combine the many tools and techniques and not solely rely on meds.

Here's a breakdown of some of the most frequently used medications:

1. <u>Selective Serotonin Reuptake Inhibitors (SSRIs)</u>: SSRIs are a class of antidepressant medications that are also effective in treating anxiety disorders. Depression and anxiety often go hand in hand. Commonly prescribed SSRIs include:
   - Sertraline (Zoloft)
   - Fluoxetine (Prozac)
   - Escitalopram (Lexapro)
   - Paroxetine (Paxil)
   - Fluvoxamine (Luvox)

2. <u>Serotonin Norepinephrine Reuptake Inhibitors (SNRIs)</u>: SNRIs are another class of antidepressants that are often prescribed for anxiety disorders. Examples of SNRIs include:
   - Venlafaxine (Effexor XR)
   - Duloxetine (Cymbalta)
   - Desvenlafaxine (Pristiq)
   - Levomilnacipran (Fetzima)

3. <u>Benzodiazepines</u>: Benzodiazepines are fast-acting medications that provide short-term relief from anxiety symptoms. However, they can be addictive and are generally prescribed for short-term use or as needed only. Taking too many benzodiazepines or taking them for a long period of time can actually increase anxiety symptoms. Common benzodiazepines include:
   - Alprazolam (Xanax)
   - Lorazepam (Ativan)
   - Clonazepam (Klonopin)

- Diazepam (Valium)

4. <u>Buspirone (BuSpar)</u>: Buspirone is an anti-anxiety medication that works by affecting serotonin and dopamine receptors in the brain. It is often used as an alternative to benzodiazepines due to its lower risk of dependence.

5. <u>Beta Blockers</u>: While primarily used to treat high blood pressure and heart conditions, beta blockers can also be helpful in managing the physical symptoms of anxiety, such as rapid heart rate and trembling. Common beta blockers include:
   - Propranolol (Inderal)
   - Atenolol (Tenormin)
   - Metoprolol (Lopressor)
   - Bisoprolol (Zebeta)

6. <u>Hydroxyzine (Vistaril, Atarax)</u>: Hydroxyzine is an antihistamine medication that is sometimes prescribed off-label for the treatment of anxiety. It works by blocking certain neurotransmitters in the brain, leading to sedative and anxiolytic (anxiety-reducing) effects. Hydroxyzine is often used for short-term relief of anxiety symptoms and may also help improve sleep quality. It is available in both oral and injectable forms.

7. <u>Gabapentin (Neurontin)</u>: Gabapentin is an anticonvulsant medication that is sometimes used off-label to treat anxiety disorders. While its exact mechanism of action in treating anxiety is not fully understood, gabapentin is thought to modulate the

release of certain neurotransmitters in the brain, including gamma-aminobutyric acid (GABA), which has a calming effect. Gabapentin is typically used as an adjunctive treatment for anxiety, particularly in individuals who have not responded adequately to other medications or therapies.

In addition to prescription medications, some over-the-counter (OTC) medications and supplements may also be used to manage anxiety symptoms. Again, always discuss taking the OTC meds with a healthcare professional because the doses and effectiveness can vary. You also may not be able to combine the OTC meds with the prescription meds. These may include:

1. <u>Antihistamines</u>: Certain antihistamines, such as diphenhydramine (Benadryl), may have mild sedative effects that can help reduce anxiety in some individuals.

2. <u>Melatonin</u>: Melatonin is a hormone that regulates sleep-wake cycles and may help improve sleep quality in individuals with anxiety-related sleep disturbances.

3. <u>Valerian Root</u>: Valerian root is an herbal supplement that has been used for centuries as a natural remedy for anxiety and insomnia. It may help promote relaxation and reduce anxiety symptoms in some people.

4. <u>L-theanine</u>: L-theanine is an amino acid found in green tea that has been shown to have calming

effects on the brain. It may help reduce anxiety and improve focus and attention.

5. <u>Magnesium</u>: Magnesium is a mineral that plays a key role in regulating neurotransmitters and may help promote relaxation and reduce anxiety symptoms when taken as a supplement.

Self-Reflection #1: Making Your Treatment Plan Unique to You

1. Review the list of all non-medication and technology techniques listed above.

2. Select one or two techniques that you could commit to practicing for two entire weeks.

3. Any time you begin a routine or add tools and techniques, I encourage you to track how you feel on a daily basis using a litmus scale of one to five, one meaning low or good, five meaning high or bad.

4. Use trackers for things such as rating sleep, mood, irritability, racing thoughts, anxious symptoms, happiness, and contentment.

5. Write down the techniques you chose and the length of time you used that technique.

6. You can use this tracking system to provide data when you visit your therapist or go to a psychiatrist or primary care doctor for a medical evaluation. They will want to know what you have tried, how it is helping or isn't, and how long you have used it.

CHAPTER EIGHT

FROM SURVIVING TO THRIVING - CRAFTING YOUR STORY OF RESILIENCE

TIME IS THE MOST precious commodity in the world. Every minute that passes is a minute you will never get back in your life. I'd bet you have been in situations you were dreading, and time moved as slowly as molasses, and that you have also had wonderful times where you were trying to cling to each second, and the moments seemed to slip through your fingers like fine, smooth sand. Time is a funny thing. However, time is all you have, and now is the time to change in your life what is no longer serving you.

This is why you need to take action now to do everything you can and learn that you are creating your own anxiety, but you learn how to manage the symptoms and alleviate the negative and debilitating impact that anxiety has in your life.

I encourage my clients to do the same thing. I've learned that anxiety will not fix itself. Read that again: anxiety does not fix itself. It just lurks around and jumps out to surprise you, keeping you in its claws. Anxiety feeds on itself, getting bigger and heavier as time goes by. In Chapter Two, I touched on what unmanaged anxiety can look like, but now I want to delve in a little deeper so the long term effects on your mind, body, and soul can hopefully motivate you to act now.

WHAT UNMANAGED ANXIETY LOOKS LIKE

Ray was a client I worked with a few years ago. He came to me because his anxiety had been spinning out of control for months. He was having panic attacks, sometimes several times a day. He wasn't sleeping, he was missing work and he was close to losing his job. Ray was forty-two years old, single, with no kids. He told me his dog was his only emotionally supportive companion.

Ray took advantage of the online therapy I had provided due to COVID. He said he may have never started therapy if he had to leave his house, so he was grateful for the option to talk to me via Zoom.

As I gathered his background information, Ray explained to me that he always remembered having a little anxiety here and there growing up, but it didn't ever seem to be problematic. However, in his midtwenties, Ray experienced an extremely traumatic event. He was sleeping in his home and woke up to smell smoke. He was able to escape from the burning apartment complex but lost most of his personal property, including items that were unreplaceable. The terror he remembers from that night never left his mind. He vividly remembers the smell, the smoke in his lungs, the heat, and the crackling of fire burning down his walls.

Ray got into counseling shortly after the fire but stopped going after a few months due to finances. He also figured he had learned the basics of how to deal with the traumatic event and felt he was ready to move on. He said he did okay, for a while, until one evening brought the trauma back to the forefront of his mind.

Ray was on the beach, enjoying himself with some friends. He hadn't planned on staying at the beach after sunset, but his friends were going to a bonfire and invited him to go. He remembered being excited to go meet new people and enjoy a party. However, once the bonfire started raging, Ray had a complete meltdown. He didn't see it coming, but the smoke and the blazing flames and the cracks and snaps of the fire hit him so hard that he went into panic.

Although he had talked about the traumatic event in therapy, he realized he hadn't worked through all the residual emotions of loss of control, fear of death, and how quickly his apartment was engulfed in flames. After that night, Ray had so much anxiety that he completely stopped going to the beach. In fact, he no longer liked the smell of the ocean, hearing the waves come in or even feeling sand on his feet.

What Ray was experiencing was tangential trauma and anxiety. Although the beach did not play a factor in that horrific night his apartment caught on fire, because he experienced panic at the beach during the bonfire, Ray began to associate the beach with the fire. Then he associated the waves, the smell of the ocean, and the sand on his feet to the beach to the bonfire, all equating back to his apartment catching on fire.

Ray's life was shrinking quickly around him. He no longer wanted to live by the beach, so he moved so far away, which is how he ended up in Colorado. However, Ray felt isolated being far away from friends and what was familiar. He began staying in his new apartment, isolating, and becoming very depressed.

As we worked together, Ray was able to identify that because he didn't deal with anxiety when it was manageable, and instead ignored the feelings of worry and fear, his mind began to associate his current situation as being a source of anxiety. I call this the "Can you hear me now?" approach.

Your body is always talking to you and will start yelling and screaming until you actually pay attention to what your body needs. Ray's body was trying to show him smaller level fears through dreams and hypervigilance to triple check that appliances were turned off, as well as hypersensitivity to smoke and heat, but Ray dismissed these small warning signs. His mind was unsettled and feeling out of control, yet Ray ignored it, telling himself he was fine.

By the time Ray went to the bonfire, his mind and body were pretty angry that Ray was ignoring their pleas to get help, so they said, "Ray, can you hear us now?" and there came the full-on panic attack. Because Ray still hadn't sought out help, he avoided the anxiety, so it just got bigger and harsher. It took Ray uprooting his life, continually having panic attacks, and almost losing his job because he couldn't make it to work, even online (because of COVID), to get Ray to call me.

Ray and I worked together to break down all the aspects of anxiety—fear, loss of control, and cognitive distortions—and he eventually developed healthy coping mechanisms. We did yoga therapy and took a mindfulness approach so Ray could develop a relationship with his body and mind where he was more in sync instead of fighting its communication between its parts.

Ray stayed in Colorado, but he has been able to go back to his hometown to visit friends and even spend time at the beach.

I give you Ray's success story because it drives home the point that if you ignore the feelings your body and mind are begging you to pay attention to, the negative emotions will only get stronger and make a larger impact on your life.

Now is the time to take action and seek out the help you need. Spend time reading and rereading this book, practicing all of the Self-Reflection activities, and be honest with yourself about what you need to do to find peace in your life.

LONG-TERM EFFECT OF UNMANAGED ANXIETY ON THE BODY AND BRAIN

Stress kills. I know it's harsh, but that is the reality. I believe in today's society, we are pushed to the edge on a daily basis. While we can handle more stress today than we could one hundred years ago, it doesn't mean we are handling stress in a healthy way.

We covered the more immediate effects that stress and anxiety have on our body and mind earlier in this book. But now, I want to look at what stress and anxiety can do to your body if not managed over a longer period of time.

Here are some statistics to get this conversation going:

1. According to Healthline, these findings were listed in an article called "Insomnia on the Rise? Use of Sleeping Pills Doubles in U.S."[4]:
   a. "The percentage of people using sleeping pills in the U.S. has doubled since 2010, according to a new study."
   b. "About 8.4% of adults use[d] sleeping pills in 2023 according to the CDC."
   c. "Dr. Thomas Kilkenny, DO, the director of the Institute Sleep Medicine at Staten Island University Hospital, believe[d] stress is to blame. 'Stress from family life, financial stresses,

---

4   Julia Ries, "Insomnia on the Rise? Use of Sleeping Pills Doubles in U.S.," Healthline, January 26, 2023, https://www.healthline.com/health-news/insomnia-on-the-rise-use-of-sleeping-pills-doubles-in-u-s.

illness especially with the COVID pandemic all can alter one's ability to fall and stay sleep,' Kilkenny, who was not involved in the study, told Healthline."

d. "Research from 2021 [details found in the article] found that the vast majority of Americans (84%) experienced significant stress."

We've already discussed how a lack of sleep can trigger more anxiety, and more anxiety can contribute to less sleep. Sleep is a basic need, and unhealthy sleep patterns have harsh long-term effects.

2. According to the Cleaveland Clinic Health Essentials article called "10 Strange Things Stress Can Do to Your Body"[5]:

a. A direct quote I found to sum the effect of stress on the body stated: "While it may feel like stress is only occurring inside your head, it's absolutely having an effect on the rest of your body. 'Stress doesn't necessarily cause certain conditions, but it can make the symptoms of those conditions worse,' says [internal medicine physician] Dr. [Richard] Lang[,MD, MPH]. 'When physical symptoms worsen, they may, in turn, increase a person's level of stress, which results in a vicious cycle.'"

---

[5] "10 Strange Things Stress Can Do to Your Body", Cleveland Clinic Health Essentials, last modified February 8, 2023, https://health.clevelandclinic.org/things-stress-can-do-to-your-body.

b. In summary, the article discusses the ways stress can show up in your body that may surprise you. These include, but are not limited to, hair loss, skin rashes, unhealthy heart and lungs, muscles and joint pain, unhealthy digestive system, pain in the shoulders, head and jaw from tension, a compromised immune system, inconsistent menstrual cycles causing an unhealthy reproductive system and hormone imbalance, extreme weight gain or weight loss, and of course, mental health instability.

The article does a good job going into detail but speaks of the fact that stress and anxiety endured over a long period of time will affect every part of your body and mind. If you experienced all or any of these symptoms, would that cause more stress? Of course it would, which will further break down the body and mind.

HUMANS ARE NOT MACHINES

On those super anxiety-ridden days, don't you wish you could just dump all your worries into the garbage disposal, pour some bleach down there, run the water and grind it all down to nothing while you hear it draining out of the pipes? Me too. But guess what? No such luck. Humans are not computers where you can put all your stress and worries into the recycle bin and click delete. The negative emotions pile up in our body, and they have to go somewhere. We either internalize the emotions or we externalize them.

Either way, over a longer period of time, there are some negative consequences of unmanaged negative anxiety.

Internalized

When we internalize anxiety, we stuff it down, ignore it, and compensate for it. Again, it doesn't go away. But as it ferments way down in our innards, it leaves its mark. We just explored the ways the body demonstrates that this internalized anxiety manifests itself.

In addition, our cognitive thought process is compromised, and over time, we can doubt ourselves to the extent of developing imposter syndrome. Imposter syndrome is when we believe other people will eventually see that we are incapable and overall stupid. Of course, this is a cognitive distortion because no one is telling us we are incapable and stupid, but internalized anxiety warps our perception of reality. Just think how this could hold you back from seeking a promotion you are fully qualified for or taking that risk to ask out that attractive person you have been admiring from a distance. There are so many ripple effects of not taking that first step because your perception is that you simply can't.

Ultimately, depression and anxiety when left untreated can lead to thought of suicide and even completing suicide. Almost always, this is preventable. Life is meant to be lived to its fullest potential, and internalizing anxiety for years and years is simply wasting time.

Externalized

When we externalize anxiety, we typically push people away or burn them out with our constant need for reassurance. Over time, not showing up to functions we promised we'd attend, being irritable and angry towards others, and having a general negative vibe will only lead to conflict and eventually to loneliness. This loneliness can also become internalized with effects becoming very serious.

START NOW TO CREATE LONG-TERM HEALTHY HABITS

In the last chapter, I gave you several ways to deal with the symptoms of anxiety. Now, I want to help you implement a way to create habits today, which, once ingrained, will set you up for long-term success in becoming more confident and able to take charge of your emotions, instead of them taking charge of you.

If you have read my first book, *Preparing for the Jungle: Avoiding Snakes and Pitfalls on the Path to Healthy Love*, you may be familiar with the Whole Life Grid. This grid breaks down your life into nine main areas: Work, Family, Friends, Primary Relationship, Alone/ Spiritual, Personal Growth, Exercise/ Health, Hobbies, and Service/ Giving Back. In *Preparing for the Jungle*, I help people understand exactly what life would look like if they were content in each area. This helps them create their ideal relationship, create nonnegotiables, and set the stage to attract healthy love.

Sometimes, when my clients first see the grid, they become a little overwhelmed. But as I've reiterated through this book, slow your pace, and take things one step at a time. Worthwhile endeavors take time. What overwhelms you as you look at your life is not having a starting place. Rachel, a former client, shared with me that she often hears people say that once she becomes whole within herself or does the inner work, she'll finally experience a sense of peace and connection with others. She said that was the most overwhelming thing she'd ever heard because she had no idea where to even start. So, she stayed stuck, repeating the same behaviors and routines that didn't serve her and hoping for a different outcome. The different outcome didn't ever come. The same outcomes were anxiety and self-doubt.

There are several ways to use the Whole Life Grid. When it comes to anxiety, I've created a road map for you to follow.

Self-Reflection #1: Whole Life Grid

1. Get a piece of unlined paper and turn it horizontally. Create your grid following the diagram you see here.

2. The first task is to take one square at a time and brainstorm aspects of this item where you had a struggle but overcame it. For example, under the "Work" topic, you may have been confused on a task item, but you asked questions, did research, completed a training, and now the task item is easier because you learned what to do. Or maybe you hated your job but felt stuck and couldn't quit because you have a family and bills to pay. But the dead-end job was creating panic attacks. You shifted your thinking and used the job as a means to pay for different training and certifications. This helped you become more qualified for a different position within the company. You are now working in a field that more suits your personality and lifestyle.

The goal is to understand that you have had struggles in your life, in each of these areas, but you have found a way to organize your thoughts and behavior around the struggle. You took charge and figured out a way to cope or change the situation.

When we have anxiety, our confidence decreases, and we tend to forget that we have struggled before. Because you are here reading this book, somehow you found a way to figure life out in those chaotic moments. You found the energy, the hope, and here you are, wanting to make changes to feel better.

3. Now move to the next square, "Family." What are some challenges you endured within your family? This could be as you were growing up or in your current family situation. How did you work through those? Did you leave? Did you stay and resolve the conflict? Did you recreate boundaries? Did you lower your expectations? You did something, and then ask yourself what you learned. Some people grow up in a family where they learn exactly what not to do when they have a family of their own. That is progress. That is taking your trials and tribulations and learning from them, applying today what you have learned. That is the 90%.

4. Continue moving through the squares. This is not a situation where you will sit down and complete the reflection in one shot. Sometimes people work on one square a day. Sometimes, people set the timer for ten minutes and do a brainstorming mind dump and fill in as much as they can in ten minutes. Then they take a break and come back to it later. Again, there is no right way to fill this grid out and recognize your past conflicts and how you managed through them. The point is to get writing. If you run out of space, grab your journal and make one topic item one journal entry and just write.

5. After you are done, take a highlighter and color over all of the achievements you have made in each section. I'm guessing you will have a very colorful page. You are a warrior. You aren't meant to just muddle through the muck of anxiety and self-doubt. It is time to take charge and make small shifts.

I highly recommend *Atomic Habits: An Easy & Proven Way to Build Good Habits & Break Bad Ones* by James Clear. I absolutely love his method of setting short-term, attainable goals and how your small habits now form long-term habits in life. Creating a new way of living isn't hard; it's just different from what isn't working. After a while, you realize you are the only one holding you back from feeling a sense of control and elevated confidence in your life.

Self-Reflection #2: Whole Life Grid with Gratitude

1. Now, get a new piece of unlined paper, turn it horizontally again, and create your grid.
2. Now set the timer for ten minutes and brainstorm in each area the things that you are grateful for. What events, people, ideas, actions, situations have come along in your life that have given you a sense of gratitude in each square?
3. You are welcome to spend longer than ten minutes if you want to because this exercise will inevitably bring a sense of calm to your nervous system. It is

almost impossible to feel gratitude and anxiety at the same time.

4. You may also use each square as a daily journal entry and elaborate on these sections.

Hang these two Whole Life Grids you've made up on a wall in your home that you frequently pass. Review them, remind yourself of the sense of accomplishment you have experienced as well as the gratitude you have in the present moment. You may even hang a pen next to these grids so as you pass by and have new memories of any aspect of gratitude, you can continue to add to the list.

Self-Reflection #3: Whole Life Grid with Reflection of Energy

1. Once again, create a new grid on a new sheet of unlined paper.

2. Set your timer for ten minutes and brainstorm the following topics, writing your answers down in the allotted square.

    a. How much energy do you spend in each square on the grid? For example, do you spend ten to twelve hours a day in your job? Are you on the job for a typical eight hours, but spend time at home in the evening replying to emails, or creating spreadsheets? Do you speed through dinner with your family and jump on the computer to finish a project with a timeline? Once in a while, that work ethic may be unavoidable, but how often does this happen? If only periodically, it may feel good to be productive and complete tasks from the day. However, if you don't find work-life balance, that may be an example of negative, stressful, or anxious energy spent in the work section.

How much energy do you spend in the personal growth section? Do you start reading a book that you find fascinating and want to continue, but something always gets in the way, and you never get to complete the book? Is your goal to complete a triathlon, but it seems someone always needs your attention, and you feel anxiety about choosing a goal for yourself or being there for someone else?

Or maybe your goal is to complete a triathlon, and you have set up a specific training schedule that requires you to spend the majority of your free time training, but it is something that brings you immense satisfaction. That would be an example of positive, motivating, or exciting energy.

b. What is your ROI (return on investment) of the energy you spend in this specific area of your life? Write positive or negative. In the examples above, the ROI with the energy you spend at work is likely not sustainable over a long period of time. Analyze the ROI for each square and determine, if you continue at this pace, will this create more anxiety or more peace in your life?

c. Paying attention to the negative ROI that you have uncovered, what are some short-term habits that you could put into place to slowly start shifting the negative ROI into positive ROI?

For example, sticking with the work topic. You may realize that this intense work schedule is short term, so you plan a short vacation after you meet your deadlines. You commit to the grind, but you see the light at the end of the tunnel, so it makes the hard work now pay off later.

You may realize that the grind at work is the culture, and that expectation is never going to change. Again, what are some habits that you can start to place into your life to manage this situation? Quitting today is probably not the best option because that could create even more anxiety than you already feel. But you could create boundaries. You take your lunch break outside of the office. You create a peaceful transition from the time you shut the computer off and the time you begin your personal evening. Instead of drowning yourself in social media or binging on Netflix over the weekend, you carve out time to update your resume, connect with recruiters, get active on LinkedIn. Set an hour on Saturday and an hour on Sunday, and then when you have completed this, you can watch some Netflix.

See, you are recognizing what is not working in your life and making small, realistic shifts. Review the previous chapter and adopt some of the non-medication coping techniques. Get creative.

d. Find a day timer or planner. I use the Panda Planner. It is sectioned into three parts: a typical calendar view with squares for each day, a weekly breakdown where I can write down my daily tasks, and a section for goals, dreams, what worked last month and what I want to do differently next month. It has several other little prompts so I can get very specific on what habits I am implementing in my life. I don't know about you, but I need to write things down to hold myself accountable. Forming new habits is tough, but as they create a positive ROI, they become easier to stick with.

CHAPTER NINE

EPILOGUE

SO, MY FRIEND, IT is time to cast your net. You have everything you need right here in this book to be able to identify, manage, process through, face, change, prevent, and take charge of the anxiety you experience.

You may be at the end of this book, but I'm not going anywhere. I always love hearing from my readers about what they are working on, how their progress is going, and if I can help out in any way. Please consider joining my private Facebook group, "Overcoming Waves: Crucial Tactics to Survive the Riptides of Anxiety." You can also visit my website www.healthyheality.net or reach out to me via email tami@healthyhealing.net.

I have so much faith that you are set on your way to find internal peace and live a life filled with contentment. Remember, anxiety will pop up because it is just an emotion. But, armed with all the tools and techniques you have learned, when you can manage the symptoms, you can regain control of your life.

ABOUT THE AUTHOR

TAMARA KIEKHAEFER IS A seasoned psychotherapist with twenty-five years of experience in private practice. Having struggled with anxiety and panic attacks throughout her life, she cracked the code on managing anxiety symptoms and is passionate about sharing her simple yet transformative techniques. Tamara has taught thousands of clients how to regain control over their anxiety, changing lives in the process.

She is the author of *Preparing for the Jungle: Avoiding Snakes and Pitfalls on the Path to Healthy Love* and has contributed to prominent publications such as *Forbes*, *Biz World*, *CEOWorld*, *Elephant Journal*, *Medium Magazine*, *Nashville Fit*, and *Gen20*. Tamara co-hosts the podcast *Unguarded Minds* with Desiree Grimaldi and manages two private Facebook groups, including *Overcoming Waves: Crucial Tactics to Survive Riptides of Anxiety*. She is also the creator of an online course Get Relationship Ready.

Tamara is married with two amazing kids, and her work continues to inspire and help people navigate the complexities of anxiety and relationships.